PUBLIC GOODS

Expecting the Best in Ethical Rigor, Moral Excellence, and Civic Engagement from America's Independent Schools

Peter Gow

LICENSING AND COPYRIGHT

.epub ISBN: 978-1-7342479-1-6

.pdf ISBN: 978-1-7342479-2-3

.mobi ISBN: 978-1-7342479-3-0

Paperback ISBN: 978-1-7342479-7-8

ABOUT THE AUTHOR

Peter Gow has been a teacher and an administrator in independent schools for over 40 years. He grew up on the campus of The Gow School and graduated from Nichols School in Buffalo, New York, before attending college at Yale and graduate school at Brown. He taught at The Gow School, Providence Country Day School, The Fessenden School, and Beaver Country Day School. He was a founding board member and then executive director of the Independent Curriculum Group and joined One Schoolhouse as Independent Curriculum Resource Director when the ICG merged with One Schoolhouse in 2019. Peter has written, consulted, and presented for schools and national educational organizations in the United States and Canada.

TABLE OF CONTENTS

PROLOGUE

It's no secret to anyone in the biz or who knows me at all that I was literally born and bred in independent schools. When my mother brought me home from the hospital at age five days, I was living in a school building, although the conversion of the upstairs into a small dormitory wouldn't happen for a few years. My father went across the street to breakfast in the Main Building every day, and he dropped by to have coffee at his mother's house at recess. In the meantime, her husband, my grandfather, stayed in his classroom/study, smoking up a storm and working with his students. They were "his" because it was his school; he'd founded it, and he owned it, back in the era of small proprietary schools.

I'm glad that era is over. I still feel a frisson of discomfort when I acknowledge that my own education was paid for out of the "net" from that school, which stopped being a family business just in time for my own arrival as a haggard grad school survivor to set up a development office and maybe even do a bit of teaching. These days I don't much care for the profit motive when it intersects with education, and a couple of the essays in this collection address the "outsourcing" issue as well as my contempt for the for-profit charter industry. Anything that looks interesting to venture capitalists should not be anywhere near children and schools, in my opinion.

"I believe that children are our future." This is a self-evident truism as well as a lyric that kind of cloys, and I also believe in most of the other truisms along the same line, especially the idea that a society should be judged by the way it treats its children.

Our society, here in the fall of 2019, isn't getting a very good report card from me. We have enacted child labor laws and offer free public education, sure, but what have we been doing truly to prepare our children to live and thrive in a world of justice, equity, security, and peace? More to the point, what have we done to offer them that world of justice, equity, security, and peace?

As I write this, the shame that young environmental activist Greta Thunberg has called down upon us is still echoing, but for how long? Some of us remember and try to take to heart the messages of Malala Yousefzai, the Ferguson protests, and then the Parkland students, and we try in our own lives to live up to the ideals and examples their advocacy and anguish represent. Individuals do have some power, perhaps most importantly the power to hope and to try to embody our hopes in our words and deeds.

Institutions have more power, but they need to name and acknowledge it. At some point it dawned on thick me that independent schools could and should be more than just a consumer upgrade tagged with terms like "excellence" and exclusivity.

You see, there must have been a reason, a couple of centuries ago, when the laws were enacted perpetually exempting St. Grottlesex and Graceful Meadows Country Day from taxation and a whole lot of programmatic regulation, laws that also offer tax relief to their donors. Is all this just some lovely special benefit for those who can afford to be a part of these places? Shouldn't independent schools be more than just a consumer upgrade tagged with terms like "excellence" and exclusivity.

Was there not a hope way back when that these institutions might actually provide a reciprocal benefit to society, a positive public good? And not just the benefit of having provided leaders in the economy and the government with an especially "fine" (as we are so often told) education, as many schools claim or at least imply when they proclaim the roll of their illustrious alums?

What about the work and posture of the schools themselves? How might they proactively harness themselves to society, to move the culture forward not just for their own students and community?

In this book I present and offer at least a preliminary exploration of multiple fronts on which I believe independent schools could act for the benefit of society. With their relative affluence, their programmatic freedoms, and above all their engaged, relational cultures of living and learning, independent schools, I believe, could and even should be working to

➢ Create and further a robust and mutually beneficial conversation involving all sectors of the K–12 educational community, with the express goal of improving the educational experiences of all students;

➢ Become active test beds for educational development for students of all ages with a focus on making the learning process more relevant and meaningful as well as more engaging;

➢ Take the lead in transforming what is now a hurtful "stress culture" in relation to college admission and access into a healthier, more invigorating process of growth and self-discovery;

➢ Become models of diversity, equity, and inclusion in their own communities, programs, policies, and practices relating to student life and especially to curriculum and instruction; and

➢ Promote the idea that advocacy and the development of core beliefs and awareness of social issues is an essential educational value.

Like its companion volume *"Past Master"*, *Public Goods* is offered as a booster shot for educators and schools in need of a little more of the courage of their own convictions.

NOTES ON THE TEXT: These essays first appeared as free-standing blog posts here and there. In preparing this e-book

I have made editorial updates and corrections so that I can stand by what I wrote as my truth in 2020. The original sources are cited after each essay, and the original posts are still available online as of this writing.

St. Basalt's School has been my generic name for "any independent school" for years.

I subscribe to the use of gender-free general pronouns, including the singular "they" and "themself." These are real things these days, even if old Grammar Police may be stroking their nightsticks in consternation. But be prepared.

WHERE IT ALL BEGAN

By 2012 I had been blogging for some years, and I had begun to see what an echo chamber the independent school-focused blogosphere had become. I had my regular readers and occasional voices from the loyal opposition, but I was increasingly realizing that what was on my independent school-focused mind was not doing much for the world of education as a whole. I had a vague idea that some independent schools were doing things that might have positive scalability, and that in their freedom from regulation, some independent school practice might actually point the way toward new and better ways of doing the work on a truly national level. One day I sat down and wrote the following, which appeared in Education Week *and probably led to my later stint there as author of the "Independent Schools, Common Perspectives" blog through much of 2013.*

I am pleased and grateful to acknowledge here my gratitude to Education Week *and its editors for these opportunities and for their permission to republish many of those "Independent Schools, Common Perspectives" posts in this volume.*

INDEPENDENT SCHOOLS SHOULD SHARE WHAT THEY KNOW

As an independent school student, teacher, coach, adviser, administrator, and most recently parent, I've drunk deep of the message that there is a legitimate and worthy alternative to public education. In my many roles, I have seen educators toil and students struggle, and I have seen hard work pay off in myriad kinds of authentic student success.

I am well aware that not everyone sees the virtues of independent education. Our schools are called exclusive, even elitist, and over-resourced, and we are accused of merely basking in the reflected glory of family wealth that

1

guarantees our students' success. As usual, though, popular images exaggerate reality; only a tiny portion of independent schools are hyperselective, and fewer still are heavily endowed with either new or old money. Most independent schools—and as an industry we represent an astounding spectrum of missions, cultures, and purposes—are tuition-driven and serve students with a wide range of capacities from families who work hard for their money. Most schools also happen to offer generous financial aid.

In any event, I'm not here to plead the case for independent schools; they can do that for themselves.

Instead, I want to issue a challenge, primarily to independent schools and their leaders, but also to public school educators.

Some background: For the last 20 or so years, from an independent school perspective, the public sector has staggered under a succession of regulatory measures that appear misguided at best and at worst downright punitive toward teachers, schools, and above all students, especially in the most economically disadvantaged districts. The national conversation on education has focused on "failing" schools, allegedly incompetent teachers, and disaffected and disengaged communities of students and parents—as if these were somehow the norm. I don't believe they are, but politicians have made hay on the issue, which now seems to have been "resolved" across the board by an oppressive regime of standardized testing, with teacher "evaluation" and even school funding based on scores. High stakes, indeed.

During these same two decades, independent schools have been awakening from what, we must admit, was a kind of programmatic lethargy dating from an earlier, less educationally illustrious era. In this recent period, our best classrooms have become hotbeds of such practices as project- and problem-based learning; student collaborations; the intensive development of technology as a tool for teaching and learning; active civic engagement; intensive science, technology, engineering, and mathematics, or STEM, programming; and new forms of classroom and overarching assessment—all undertaken against the rigorous standards imposed de facto by a competitive marketplace.

Leading schools have embraced every aspect of every enumeration of "21st-century skills" as major learning objectives, with creativity and innovation at the core of all. Perhaps not surprisingly, some of the most established and well regarded of the "old schools"—places that could coast on their reputations for decades to come—have begun to use their prestige to leverage vaulting change in the way they teach and construct learning experiences for their students.

Innovation has become the byword, at least aspirationally, in independent education, but not, praise be, at the expense of the more traditional values that have characterized independent schools. A century before there were charter schools built around cherished principles of curriculum or character education, in dependent schools were forming themselves around curricular and affective missions and core values that still define individual schools—perhaps even more sharply in 2012 than they may have done in 1912, thanks to a renewed emphasis on these outcomes as elements of the student experience at each school. Successful independent schools take the concept of "student centered" as a mantra, an obligation—and again, the harsh realities of a highly competitive market compel independent schools to walk the walk, if they are to thrive.

Our schools are not perfect, and no one should claim that they are. But independent schools are by and large delivering on a number of promises in areas of academic and affective (and in the case of schools with faith-based heritages or missions, spiritual) learning and development that experts tell us are critical to the creation of the flexible, creative, ever-learning, active citizenry and workforce that our world will need to meet the daunting conditions of the future.

And so, my challenge: It's time for a true national dialogue in which independent school educators take the lead in sharing the lessons we have been learning in recent years. The other parties to this dialogue must be public and other kinds of schools.

It's time for independent schools to assert their way as a body into the larger conversation on education, locally, severally, and nationally. We need to start talking about ourselves as places of teaching and learning, gently pushing aside assumptions of prestige and focusing on what we truly know about educating children. Many of our schools have embraced the idea of their public purpose, and here is a way to express that purpose in a manner that transcends even the most ambitious local or regional partnerships aimed at community service, tutoring, or professional development.

It's also time for public school leaders—and I realize that this may be asking a great deal of men and women with little time to spare—to ask independent schools, perhaps even to demand of us, how we might be of service. It's easy to say that independent school people just don't get it, but we have to try, and public-sector educators have to help us—and to try to understand us. In the real world we occupy, independent schools aren't going to just empty their coffers into the till of public education, declare themselves deceased, and bring about an instant Finland with great public schools for every child and no private education.

What independent schools have to contribute, I think, are ideas—ideas on effective ways to deliver high-quality, high-standards learning experiences to all kinds of students. No, we're not perfect, and not every one of our best practices can be replicated. But for a while now we have had the luxury, if you will, of being able to implement, unfettered by politics, new practices based on new understandings of how children learn and grow, and I believe we have a public obligation to share our experiences.

I don't quite know how this dialogue should start—a series of colloquia, perhaps, or maybe a giant conference. In time, I would hope to see teachers talking to teachers across sector frontiers in ways that are only too rare right now. The time is right.

I don't imagine that my cry for dialogue here is going to change everything overnight. But we are all educators together, and we all believe in children and in the future. I can't make myself not believe that we can and will learn from one another. Independent schools have plenty to learn, but the dialogue for which I am calling needs to be based on a recognition—by ourselves, above all—that we also have something to teach.

"Commentary," *Education Week*, August 28, 2012

THE #PubPriBridge: INDEPENDENT SCHOOLS AND THE COMMUNITY OF EDUCATORS

Some years ago I was part of a small but active movement among a small group of independent school people to try to build connections between our world and the worlds of public school and other educators. For a while we hosted a Twitter chat to which we gave the inelegant name, #PubPriBridge. We didn't succeed in expanding the movement much, but we were able to offer a panel session at the 2015 National Association of Independent Schools Annual Conference that featured educational leaders from public and public charter schools as well as the late John Chubb, at that time the president of NAIS.

This section is offered to illuminate some of the thinking behind the #PubPriBridge idea. Its placement first in this volume is intended to put a stake in the ground and raise upon it the flag of intersector collaboration.

1

ABOUT #PUBPRIBRIDGE: WHAT IT IS AND WHAT WE HOPE FOR

#PubPriBridge supports a Twitter chat bringing together a community of educators interested in building authentic connections between public and independent school teachers and leaders.

The originators of #PubPriBridge are independent school educators united here by a belief that strong public schools are the backbone of a durable democratic society and that our independent school community ought to be a strong voice in support of excellent education for all children in all schools.

#PubPriBridge is the product of many conversations among independent school friends about how we, as independent school educators, might join other educators from the public school world in conversations on education. It emerges from an aspiration to build bridges of significance between educators across sectors.

The originators have some profound hopes for #PubPriBridge:

That we might begin to talk about what we all know to be true about education and how best to serve students.

That such conversations might inspire independent school teachers to become more connected to one another, to public school peers, and to the broader national and even global conversation about education.

That such conversations might inspire public school teachers to become more connected to one another, to public school peers, and to the broader national and even global conversation about education.

That these conversations might help set a direction for a new kind of inter-sector partnership of educators toward the goal, as expressed by former National Association of Independent Schools president Pat Bassett, of fortifying a mutual commitment "to make the waves that raise all boats."

That we might direct these waves toward helping all students in all schools rise higher, think more deeply, and become more engaged and active citizens.

That in participating in these conversations we shall enact our civic duty to connect, to speak out, and to honor our shared calling as educators.

That we not mire ourselves down in endless critique of what isn't working in our society's efforts at changing the nature of education and of schools, and that we focus instead on what can and must work.

We hope to see you join us at the #PubPriBridge chat!

#PubPriBridge, February 4, 2014

2

WHAT THE INDEPENDENT SCHOOL–PUBLIC SCHOOL DIALOGUE NEEDS

I have reiterated my message that America's independent schools not only know a few things about 21st-century education but also have a kind of civic obligation to pass along their knowledge in partnership—reciprocal partnership, it must be emphasized—with educators in other K–12 sectors.

This seems clear to me. As one commenter on an earlier post observed, all educators who care about kids have a responsibility to share best practices and promising approaches with one another. As the commenter noted, education "isn't, in its general practice, proprietary," and blogs, journals, and even tweets transmit ideas on practice in a non-stop river of information.

But educators know that authentic dialogue is the way people learn best, and there are many fewer opportunities for educators from different sectors to sit face-to-face with one another and talk shop. Some disciplinary conferences have a strong independent school presence, but the largest conferences tend to be so focused on public school practices and needs (or so independent school people seem to believe) that independent school folks tend to shy away, looking to spend their time and professional development dollars on events aimed at the unique (we sometimes believe) issues of our own sector.

Independent schools are missing a bet here: a larger presence at large-scale events and a more assertive effort to create and lead or otherwise participate in learning sessions at events like the ASCD or ISTE national conferences would be welcome. I don't think that relatively low independent school participation at these conferences is rooted in arrogance or aloofness; it is far more a matter of diffidence about entering into those massive conversations or maybe even that we have convinced ourselves that our situations are so idiosyncratic that other educators won't be interested. We need to get over this and step up, present company included. The worst the organizers can say is no, but I suspect that is no more likely to happen to an independent school-originated proposal than to anyone else's.

We are finding, slowly, avenues for bringing independent school and public school educators together at the teacher-to-teacher level. Many independent school educators have found the EdCamp model to be ideal for this sometimes revelatory work, and I urge my independent school confreres to use EdCamps explicitly to open inter-sector conversations. I have yet to hear a report from one of these sessions that does not include a great deal of warmth and even pleasant surprise as teachers work through misconceptions and stereotypes toward authentic conversations about their students and their work. Turns out that when teachers get together they pretty quickly find a common perspective: the desire to talk about kids and teaching.

For the past few months I have joined with a couple of like-minded independent school folks, Laura Robertson and Chris Thinnes, to offer a Twitter chat, the #PubPriBridge, through which we have tried to gin up some inter-sector conversation. We have discussed teacher evaluation, place-based learning, standardized testing, the nature of effective independent-public school partnerships, and other topics on which every educator has at least an opinion. The conversations have been small, intimate one might say, but there is a certain purity and a quiet joy in just chit-chatting with colleagues across the continent about teacher stuff—even in 140-character snippets.

#PubPriBridge is one thing and the EdCamp movement is another, but we need a more comprehensive approach. Independent schools extol and cleave to their mission statements, and I'd like to see an organization, or a series of events, whose stated purpose would be to bring educators together across all sectors to build and fortify, to lift some language from the #PubPriBridge statement of purpose, "a mutual commitment 'to make the waves that raise all boats'" and to "direct these waves toward helping all students in all schools rise higher, think more deeply, and become more engaged and active citizens."

Educational organizations are proliferating these days, and I seem to be calling here for one more, or at the very least for an existing group or consortium to put itself behind a systematic effort to create more spaces—in "real life" and through publication and communication—to bring together the men and women (and perhaps even their students!) whose work toward the common goal of teaching kids is all too often isolated into silos by differences in school structure and governance and whose worlds are further sundered by (always) perceptions and (often) realities of socioeconomic and cultural difference; but these differences and perceptions, once acknowledged and addressed, are not barriers to real dialogue.

This effort will take leadership, resources, and will. I'm not worried about an overall lack of any of these, but there must emerge a catalyst to galvanize this effort into being, a power beyond my poor words and even the earnest voices of #PubPriBridge.

But bringing educators together to share with one another is a task worth doing, and worth doing well.

"Independent Schools, Common Perspectives," *Education Week*, May 22, 2014

3

BUILDING THE PUBLIC-PRIVATE SCHOOL BRIDGE: A CONSTRUCTION UPDATE

On rare occasions it is vouchsafed to us that something important in our lives should be truly important to others. This week a former student wrote a little disquisition for the *Atlantic* online on the matter of how educators in different sectors ought to be connecting with one another in order to expand and more fully inform the conversation on teaching, learning, and education policy.

Some days I find myself trying to straddle parallel tracks in my own life, and perhaps I work too hard sometimes to keep things separated. *Not Your Father's School* has occasionally touched but I believe seldom dwelt on my own interest in bringing the independent school world into contact with our brothers and sisters in public education, and yet a fair portion of my working thought is focused on this topic, as poor a hand as I have been at actually bringing this kind of connection into being. A year ago I joined my friends Chris Thinnes from California and Laura Robertson from Virginia to put together a bi-weekly Twitter chat under the hashtag #PubPriBridge, and we keep a website that supports and complements the chat.

The *Atlantic* piece, by David Cutler (himself an independent school teacher), makes reference to #PubPriBridge, and perhaps the piece will breathe a bit more life into what has been a lively but rather limited conversation. I note that the majority of our participants are from independent schools, which suggests to me a yearning from this side of the industry but which also highlights the challenges of building the eponymous bridge. Cutler's article covers other bases, too, from the possibilities for inter-sector conversation inherent in the EdCamp model and the voice of the NAIS president,

John Chubb, who has rather courageously suggested that independent schools are not always the *ne plus ultra* of educational practice that we are sometimes believed (often, alas, in the less reflective corners of our own communities) to be.

Stereotypes and assumptions pose huge barriers to erecting the #PubPriBridge and sending a steady flow of conceptual traffic across it, and it will take time to break these down on both sides. Leadership will also be important; John Chubb is a strong presence in the conversation, but there will need to be others from both the public and independent school worlds for whom this is an important project, worthy of time and energy and the assembling of resources.

In my mind there would be an event, a special gathering of people specifically interested in this work, with some strong voices as keynotes but much, much opportunity for dialogue, shallow and deep. May as well get to the stereotypes as well as the deeper policy issues or questions about pedagogy; it's all part of the discussion.

In the meantime, we of the #PubPriBridge founding corps are pleased to remind readers here that we're taking the show on the road over the next few months. At the NAIS Annual Conference we will be part of a panel on the dialogue question, along with Pam Moran, superintendent of the Albemarle County Public School system in Virginia, educational advocate Karen Aka of Hawai'i's Academy 21, and Diana Smith, principal of the Washington (DC) Latin Public Charter School—and moderated by none other than John Chubb. In March we'll be in San Francisco presenting at the <u>Private Schools with Public Purpose Conference</u>. You can find the details on our presentations on <u>our blog</u>.)

To tie another couple of threads in my life together, I will be representing myself and my own perspectives at these events, although it is my fond hope that the Independent Curriculum Group, which has counted a few public high schools among its members, might be a conduit through which cross-sector conversations might flow in the future as they have, in a small way, in the past.

In the meantime, we'd love to have more participants on the #PubPriBridge Twitter chat. Do check the #PubPriBridge website if you'd like to learn more about the initiative.

Not Your Father's School, January 22, 2015

4

WE'RE ALL STAKEHOLDERS IN PUBLIC EDUCATION

A while ago I had a reader suggest that I lay off my expressions of empathy for public school teachers and the burdens that various policies and reform efforts have laid upon them: so-called valued-added evaluation, endless rounds of standardized testing for their students, and public excoriation at the hands of politicians and pundits on all sides.

I guess my thoughts sounded like crocodile tears. How could someone from schools like ours—independent schools: tuition-driven, self-governed, self-funding—know or care about the daily travails of public schools and their teachers and students?

Well, my direct personal experience may be limited, but I have some ideas about what is right and what is wrong for schools, teachers, and kids. I am no expert, maybe, but I've had questions about some of the structural "reforms" that have been laid upon (and, to be fair, sometimes emerged from, and then been twisted) public schools for quite a while. A few years back the late <u>Gerald Bracey's *Education Hell*</u> reaffirmed my perspective that public schools are being weakened, not strengthened, by testing-based "reforms," and <u>Diane Ravitch's stirring *The Death and Life of the Great American School System*</u> just underscored this for me. That's where I'm coming from. Forget about what kinds of schools I've been at.

I happen to believe that privatizers and corporatizers are a real threat to America's children. We're a society excited by the idea of making a buck, a giant buck, and there's a large and influential audience—outside the education field, mostly—that is thrilled when successful capitalists offer to spend their idle hours doing to schools whatever they did for their computer company or chain store. And some folks are just as intrigued when other capitalists try to turn their clever business practices—it's all about efficiencies, data, economies of scale—toward making a buck out of public education by setting up for-profit charter schools. Bedazzled, we let the money control the narrative. Dennis Sparks pretty well summed it all up in a blog post late last year.

As a society and as a national education industry (although I hate calling it that), we have the know-how to teach every kid well. We have the wealth to create schools in which every student is known, valued, and educated, although more and more of that wealth is being concentrated in the hands of a few—frankly, a few so tiny that how they choose to educate their own kids is an irrelevancy except as part of the counter-narrative.

Know-how and wealth. What's missing, of course, is the will.

Of course we have created systemic problems that have ensured that many of the nation's largest public school systems are the most at-risk. White Flight (you could call it something else) trashed city tax bases in the 60s and 70s, followed up by taxpayer rebellions that cut education funding in states starting in the 1980s. Some suburbanites may have held on to theirs, mostly, but city kids—and country kids, too, although we tend to forget about them—now often find themselves in schools with aging buildings, few resources, and teachers blamed for poor student performance that was born in impoverished homes before the kids even started school. And we ignore the obvious advantages that strong pre-school programs can give every child.

Chicago, Philadelphia, and Washington, we learn, are set to close a bunch of schools, cramming together lthousands of students, disproportionately minority in schools that are already bursting. And let's remember that during the teacher strike in Chicago last year, public school parent Matt Farmer offered up a rousing oration on what kids there, and every other kid in that city and every other community, deserve. He just happens to reference—positively—an independent school; that speech was echoing in my head when I wrote my own reminiscence on my public school years.

I am saying nothing that anyone reading this doesn't already know. And there's little in the story the way I see it that doesn't make me angry, and sad, and frustrated. I'm an educator, a taxpayer, and a citizen, and my distress for kids and teachers isn't crocodile tears.

Every parent, every teacher, every administrator, every alum, every trustee, and, yes, every student in an independent school is a stakeholder in our nation's future.

We are, in the broadest sense, all the surrogate parents of all of our nation's children. Many of us involved with independent schools have ideas about how schools are supposed to be; read this blog, listen again to Matt Farmer's references to the University of Chicago Laboratory Schools (and the righteous and proper stance of its head), go and visit an independent school in your community. We want to see democracy, not capitalism, survive as the root, stem, leaves, and fruit of American education.

"Independent Schools, Common Perspectives," *Education Week*, April 1, 2013

5

INDEPENDENT SCHOOLS AND PUBLIC SCHOOLS—IS THERE A COMMON PERSPECTIVE?

Last month Alan Jones wrote an eloquent "Commentary" essay titled "Mr. Obama: Most Schools Aren't Like Your Daughters' School." He offered a painful comparison between his observations of many public schools and the environment at the independent school attended by the First Daughters. Dr. Jones noted that many policies favored by the Obama administration, like those of preceding administrations, are likely to further dilute the quality of the student experience in public schools.

Having spent my life in independent schools, I am used to and wince at such comparisons. I was raised on the campus of a tiny school founded to teach dyslexic boys. I attended an independent school, and I have taught at four and spent working time on the campuses of many more. I know quite a bit about their aspirations and faults, their struggles and vulnerabilities.

What are "independent schools"? In the United States such schools are independent of external bodies—governments or churches, for example. Under loosened federal and state regulations they develop their own curricula and standards and fund themselves through tuitions and donations. Independent schools are full-on examples of "site-based" governance, their basic policies set and leaders hired by self-sustaining volunteer boards. A tiny handful are proprietary or for-profit and thus ineligible for membership in the National Association of Independent Schools (NAIS). NAIS also requires member schools to have "a demonstrated commitment to ethnic and economic diversity, as evident in [their] nondiscrimination policies for admission and hiring."

At a later time I will explore the variety of independent schools, but overall they represent an astonishing and stereotype-busting range of missions and cultures. All 1400 or so NAIS member schools are accredited by regional bodies working on the same principles that guide the accreditation of public schools. Most, perhaps in some contrast to that attended by the Obama children, are neither extravagantly resourced nor breathtakingly selective.

But Alan Jones is onto something important, something that troubles me and many of my independent school colleagues deeply. Public policy and debate on education these days cast a widening shadow over the work of teaching and learning. No Child Left Behind-driven testing regimes distort curricula and teaching, and over-reliance on test results to evaluate teachers and schools is misguided and damaging.

Although independent schools are "private," I am sickened by the notion of privatizing public education—especially of privatization for profit and the imposition of business-inspired "efficiencies" on children. My personal jury is still out on charter schools, however noble the basic idea and however successful many have been. Vouchers seem at the very least to offer boards of education a pernicious escape route away from making substantive improvement in the schools they are charged to operate.

Independent schools are permitted and even encouraged in this country because they offer diverse alternatives that are thought to represent a public good. These schools and those involved with them have often been stereotyped as elitist and out of touch, and historically and (alas) at present there is some truth behind the stereotype; sometimes we have forgotten why we have been permitted to exist. Some months back I spoke out in a "Commentary" piece of my own on the need for our schools to engage in the broader conversation on education—that we have much to learn and possibly even a thing or two to teach.

Independent school educators are as worried about public education as everyone else. There is no consolation for us in policies that exacerbate the differences between public and independent schools as described by Alan Jones, no celebration when public districts cut services or programs. Even when we are the incidental beneficiaries of such cutting, there is no pleasure in contemplating what schools are like for children who do not and cannot, for whatever reasons, attend ours.

I hope here mainly to focus on schools—on teaching, learning, and students, rather than on policies and politics. I also plan over time here to write more about why independent and public school educators need to interact more.

In the end I can speak only for myself, but I know that in the independent school community I am not alone in wishing that the public and independent school communities, sundered by history and economics, might better understand each other. There seem to be people eager to see the end of public education in this country, but the vast majority of independent school educators in my acquaintance are NOT among that group.

"Independent Schools, Common Perspectives," *Education Week*, February 15, 2013

6

COVERED BRIDGES: DEMOGRAPHICS, ECONOMICS, AND THE EDUCATION CONVERSATION

One of my pet projects for the past few years has been to find ways to increase the real, teacher-level discourse among educators from the private and public sectors, in all their manifold incarnations. The metaphor I and my colleagues in this endeavor has been that of a bridge—our lip-popping Twitter hashtag, #PubPriBridge, and our related website say it all. Who doesn't like bridges?

Earlier this week I took my quest over the physical Sagamore Bridge to EdCamp Cape Cod, my second time at this event held at Sandwich High School and organized by a team so efficient that it made my head spin. They had shaken the sponsor money tree so hard that one of the longest sessions was the prize giveaway at the end. And there was even fresh bread left over.

My usual session, in the case titled "What Do Private And Public School Educators Have To Say To Each Other?" drew a pretty paltry crowd—four of us in a room, representing (as teachers, former teachers, former students, and parents) every sector from parochial to charter to mainstream public to independent to home-school. The conversation was spirited, and it uncovered something that needed to be uncovered, I guess.

To put it bluntly, Cape Cod is a region of shrinking demographics for school-age children, a significant level of underemployment, and a surfeit of schools. While several public school systems have joined to regionalize, the highest-profile charter school is seeking to open a third campus, and the smallish independent schools are in a justified panic about

21

where their new students might come from. The uppermost tiers of the socioeconomic bleachers even tend to send their kids to boarding school or even to commute—something probably unthinkable before an old rail line reopened as a commuter line—to independent schools in Boston.

Two years ago at EdCamp Cape Cod the grumpy lunchtime banter among the public school teachers was about the big charter, which seemed to be drawing off the best students with its IB program and low cost. This year there was doomsday talk about the independent schools and even some of the smaller public districts. Everyone agreed that the culprit is demographics, and just this afternoon the *Boston Globe* confirmed this with a chilling feature piece titled, "Why are so many young professionals fleeing the Cape?"

Monday's conversation at EdCamp, however, took even more turns. Were the charters and some of the private schools trading on a kind of elitism? Was something referred to as "white flight"—something about which we know way too much in metro Boston—in play? Were the increasingly diverse immigrant communities scaring families with the savvy to go charter or the funds to pay for private away from the mainstream public schools? Was income inequality driving these trends faster and harder than ever? Yes, yes, yes, and yes, was the consensus, and this among educators who happened to be or to have been stakeholders in every sector. It wasn't a pretty picture being painted.

For the #PubPriBridge-building idealist in me, this was a sad conversation, as much as I learned. I knew a bit about this all from my previous EdCamp Cape Cod and from living in the region, but the hardest part was witnessing a conversation among educators that never really got to "the good stuff" about education. Wariness and fear of competition leached the teacher-talk right out of the room, even among a tiny handful of people who had come in predisposed to share and learn.

Here's what I learned, though: I "learned" what as a teacher and a citizen I already knew, that when people and interests are pitted against one another, whether by design or by overwhelming social and economic forces, what suffers is the advancement of education. Teachers, administrators, school boards, parents, and ultimately children who are forced into places of suspicion and fear aren't going to be doing as much as they could to promote or deliver or support or experience authentic, whole-child, democratic learning.

Short of an economic miracle, not much seems likely to change on the Cape in the next few years, and in the great scale of things I suppose things aren't as bad as they might be, say, in inner-city Baltimore or Ferguson, Missouri, or in the hundreds of U. S. counties where "rural poverty" dominates the landscape. In all these places, just as on picturesque Olde Cape Cod, the education conversation is derailed and twisted by economics and ill-considered policies that turn the possibilities of erecting bridges into something more like digging bunkers.

I have no cure, no solution, but if indeed "you learn something new every day," this part of my learning that day was kind of dreary. It's a good thing the rest of EdCamp Cape Cod was terrific—including the sponsor-supplied food and refreshments—and I came home as much energized as disheartened.

But as I recrossed the Sagamore Bridge and headed back toward Boston, all I could think of was that the #PubPriBridge is a lot harder to build than I think it should be, all for reasons that don't have very much to do at all with teaching and learning.

Not Your Father's School, August 6, 2015

7

INDEPENDENT–PUBLIC SCHOOL PARTNERSHIPS: EVOLVING PARADIGM, HUGE POTENTIAL

Big news at the annual conference of the National Association of Independent Schools yesterday was the debut of the National Network of Schools in Partnership, a newly formed coalition of about fifty independent schools with established working partnerships—of many shapes, sizes, histories, and purposes—with public schools.

Such partnerships aren't new, or even particularly novel, but at some point it occurred to a group of involved schools that a kind of movement was afoot, and that some sort of alliance might serve multiple purposes.

Yesterday afternoon's roll-out—more of an acknowledgment than an unveiling—was preceded by a drum-roll announcement by the outgoing NAIS president, Patrick Bassett, at the morning's annual meeting, and it was keynoted, as it were, by Maureen Dowling, director of Office of Non-Public Education at the U. S. Department of Education. According to Dowling, whose office, with participation from Secretary of Education Arne Duncan, has been tracking and supporting the formation of the partnership, "The potential of this launch is beyond anything that I've been privy to at the U. S. Department of Education." It should be noted that a Federal official is a rare sighting at one of these events.

The event included testimonials of a sort from three NNSP member independent schools and one public school head. The gist of their stories was that partnerships are do-able and, as head Todd Bland of Milton Academy said, "This is good news. This is good news for everyone, for all children." Examples ranged from teachers simply talking to each other about teaching to students working together to clean up the schools' shared neighborhood to students mentoring and even developing curriculum for each other. The message was that everyone can benefit—that successful partnerships work both ways.

A partnership can start, as head Tom Little of Park Day School in Oakland, California, observed, with independent school leaders becoming "familiar with the issues your [public school] district is facing. It's a matter of building neighborhood relationships—having kids get together and participate together." Little also cited the benefits of moving beyond what he called "private school privilege," which, like White Privilege, "is never having to think about The Other."

I had a chance to meet after the session with NNSP board member Rod Chamberlain of Kamehameha Schools in Hawaii; Claire Leheny, NNSP executive director; and board member Jacqueline Smethurst, whose Wingspan Partnerships (founded with her husband, David Drinkwater) has midwifed a number of partnerships.

Successful partnerships, according to Smethurst, follow "certain principles. The schools approach each other out of a sense of mutual interest. It is a two-way learning process, and you have to be a credible partner. It requires persistence and patience; organic growth is a hallmark." The starting point, Leheny says, is to just do it: "We can sit within our independent school contexts and worry about what public schools may or may not like, when in fact we should just engage in a conversation to find out." In the end it's about "how we can learn together," notes Chamberlain. "There are more open doors than ever." He points out that "There's a lot more of this going on than we thought, but they're all sort of in isolation"—at least up to now.

NNSP leaders acknowledge that the charge of noblesse oblige is easy to lob. "Everyone is concerned with that perception, perhaps to a fault. But if you start with reciprocity, authentic commitment to partnership, and mutually relevant work, then that goes away," says Leheny. The reality is that many independent schools have resources unavailable to public schools, and the real paradigm shift is for independent schools to start viewing themselves—and encouraging themselves to be regarded—as community resources upon which public schools might draw in specific ways, as they do with public libraries, cultural institutions, or museums.

The trick will be to develop the partnership idea to the point that the resource role is baked into independent schools' understanding of their own missions and of their public purpose. "This no longer a hidden part of that mission," adds Chamberlain.

The National Network of Schools in Partnership premiered to a packed house, and dozens of listeners requested information on membership afterward. If Maureen Dowling is right, the potential is enormous.

"Independent Schools, Common Perspectives," *Education Week*, March 1, 2013

EQUITY FROM WITHIN: RESISTING TEMPTATION

It's an unfortunate fact of life that, as Wu-Tang Clan pointed out years ago, cash rules everything around me. This is just a part of the deal that independent schools make for their very existence, depending as they must on tuition revenue, donations, and market returns on their investments. Even the tax relief granted to themselves and to their donors makes up a measurable amount of the difference between survival and closure.

Therefore, the availability of money and the cost of goods, services, and human resources is always on the minds of independent schools. Historically schools have "gone where the money is," and these schools' association with wealth, privilege, and power is not just coincidental.

In recent decades, at least, responsible educators and their schools have tried to distance themselves from their earlier image, but schools and their governing bodies and auditors can seldom operate only from the loftiest moral plane. Money, how it's made and how it's spent, must always be an operational consideration. Economies on the one hand and rich sources on the other will always offer opportunities and sometimes temptations.

In the course of almost every independent school board meeting I have ever attended, someone raises, often explicitly, the notion that "schools are businesses" and that smart operations require the adoption of "business-like practices," almost inevitably involving cutting corners on core human and even mission-aligned services. Maybe it's just clever management, garbed in the language of prudence, but too often I have seen the heart and soul of the school at risk of being eaten away. I can only sigh.

The lives of schools are about choices, and on that loftiest of moral planes can be found the criteria and the fulcrums by which and on which to balance determinations about where money will come from and where it must go. That plane, in the purest of my idealistic universes, is about mission, about the human needs of students and staff, and about the very souls of schools. Great schools cannot be selling their souls.

8

ON OUTSOURCING: LUNCH, THE NEW SAT, AND WHY WE NEED INDEPENDENT CURRICULUM

When I was a child at my father's school, the barber, the dry-cleaner, and the linen truck were the primary outside service providers. I remember the happy day Pop inked the contract with a food service company, in one gesture removing his most vexatious operational burden. Pretty much everything else was done in-house, by what in today's world would seem an absurdly tiny staff.

Most independent schools would probably concur that their first major foray into outsourcing was when they signed on with one of the outfits that now prep our salad bars and sauté our tofu—including global giants who were among the first service corporations to turn economies of scale into huge profit margins built on students. The Age of Sage then cleared the way for other, similar services—landscaping and field care, cleaning, trash and recycling, plant infrastructure support of every kind.

In the last twenty years or so a new realm has been added, professional services related to both advancement and academic program, primarily tech-intensive "solutions" to problems once addressed by administrators and staff whose institutional value was directly proportional to the number of beige filing cabinets their offices. Now, every business, development, admissions, college counseling, health, and academic office has its "key vendors," in whose servers whole schools and student bodies exist in digital form and upon whose expertise schools, faculties, students, and families rely in ways that would give them the shakes if they stopped to add it all up. As a some-time consultant, even I am an outsourced resource, though no school would fail were I or my hard-drive to melt down.

We've outsourced, we believe, to give us more time and energy to focus on things that matter, like kids and teaching and learning, although most of us would be hard pressed to point out specific areas in which a lighter clerical workload has resulted in an easier or smoother overall workflow; it has been famously noted that we're working harder than ever, even with all of the labor-saving benefits of technology. Nor have I noted any reduction in staff size at independent schools. Outsourcing has ramped up the number of our tasks and expectations about how we will perform them—better, faster, and more frequently.

But there's another bit of outsourcing we've been doing for a while, and this week's announcement of a "new and improved" SAT rather highlights this. Whatever one thinks about the SAT, new or old, its ACT cousin, or its AP step-children, it is and will be with us always. Whatever its roots, in the Common Core or in the desires of <u>the multitudes with whom the College Board's David Coleman is said to have consulted</u>, it will be debated until another revision comes along.

With large-scale standardized testing, schools have essentially been outsourcing for a century the accreditation of individual students, mirroring the not-quite-as-old outsourcing of school accreditation itself. A student's test score is a kind of seal of approval, numerically coded to show relative strength in particular areas; the debate rages and will continue as to whether these areas are "arcane vocabulary," test-prep gamesmanship, or important knowledge, but there you are. Every student from your school who sits a standardized test has been outsourced, by school and family, for judgment. (I might also point out that schools offering "Advanced Placement"-designated courses also outsource the accreditation of these courses via the review process that permits them to use the AP trademark.)

This might be an extreme way of viewing the matter; it probably is. But since the SAT and its kin aren't going anywhere soon, it's worth pondering what all this means for schools.

On the one hand we can "own" the standards and methods on which the tests are based. We can incorporate them into our practice much as you have adjusted to the wishes of your food service provider for new equipment or as your business office has clung to PCs in order to accommodate the creaky software package that now contains every transaction the school has made since 1991.

It won't be terrible to do this—many will argue, almost irrefutably, that it's the right way to support students. If the tests and the standards on which they are based—SAT, ACT, AP, SAT Subject Tests, or even the CWRA—can demonstrate that they are worthy, we'll focus a little harder on evidence-based reading, science reasoning, specific content knowledge, and performance tasks. It's what we've been doing, or often claimed and sometimes denied doing (depending on who's asking, and why), all along. But the old worry, that "teaching to a test" can divert us from core values and core mission beliefs, will remain.

Schools will still need to address yet another outsourcing question: What about test prep? Khan Academy and the SAT may now be hand-in-glove, but will that be enough for families conditioned to believe that more, and more expensive, is better? We're told that the test-prep industry is worth $4.5 billion to the American economy, and I'd bet that independent school families pay a disproportion of those dollars. Will the new SAT be enough "like school" to obviate the need for test prep? Ask families who have shelled out to tutor their children for the ACT, also described as being "like schoolwork." A great many schools now contract with outside vendors to offer standardized test prep, either as part of the freight or for an extra fee, and I suspect the new SAT will not reduce their number.

If the new SAT turns out to be everything it's cracked up to be—sight unseen—it will be a good thing, but in any case it will remain as an external validator of our students and, some would say, implicitly of our programs. Objectively, external validation is a good thing, and few would argue that independent school accreditation, for example, is actively harmful, even when it doesn't live up to its promise.

Good external validation can truly "improve the breed," and therefore we can hope that appropriate, smart standardized tests can help make schools better and bring out the best in our students—especially if schools and students are given feedback that supports better instruction and learning on a holistic basis, beyond simply achieving higher scores.

It's worth taking a moment, however, to mull over the degree to which we've passed so much of what used to be our own work to third-party vendors. In theory this should have been enabling us to focus on our core work—students and their learning and teachers and their teaching—and in sum it probably has. But take a moment, as the news cycle briefly reminds us all of the power of the College Board, to consider what all this outsourcing offers us—and what it might also take away.

Some years back the Independent Curriculum Group came together to support the development of school-based, teacher-created, mission-based curriculum and assessment. The looming of a new SAT underscores the continuing relevance of schools' efforts to draw upon their *own* resources to serve their *own* students in the best and most intentional of ways.

Food service is one thing, but our academic programs are quite another.

Not Your Father's School, March 6, 2014

9

UMBRIDGING: OUTSOURCING AND THE THREAT TO THE HEART OF SCHOOLS

I have written above about outsourcing, the tendency in schools these days to hand over responsibility for a myriad of institutional tasks to third-party vendors whose efficiencies and expertise ostensibly make it easier, and maybe cheaper, for schools to let someone else do it.

In the previous post I purposely avoided the elephant in the faculty common room, online learning. Plenty of excellent schools are outsourcing some of their instruction these days, a handful through experienced independent-school-created organizations like the Online School for Girls (since transformed into One Schoolhouse) and Global Online Academy. These providers, in particular, appeal because their credentials, and their people, are pretty well known within the independent school community; if you will, we can validate the quality of their offerings based on our own experience. (As can I with regard to the professional development offerings of O.S.G. and of Powerful Learning Practice, with which I also have personal experience.)

A raft of other vendors of online learning, however, are out there, and it's going to be a matter of trial and error to vet the ones to which we're most confidently going to send our students for that advanced math or language course that our school cannot offer.

Similarly, we are probably going to have to figure out by experience how to deal with the MOOC universe; will we grant credit or placement to a student for an EdX or Udacity badge? What about more *sui generis* MOOCs, which are popping up here and there? What will these things all mean?

There are those who cheerily view the proliferation of online learning experiences and MOOC badges as harbingers, if not proximate causes, of the death of the education system as we know it, and to some degree they may be correct. A couple of decades of experience with corporate training—a realm where online instruction is well established—have proven that concrete skills and techniques are susceptible to instruction delivered from a screen to a motivated learner, especially if the subject matter has instrumental value (as in, a new skill = a promotion or raise) to the student. Khan Academy seem to operate on this same kind of straightforward transactional psychology.

(It will be interesting, incidentally, whether the new SAT will really be quite so straightforward in itself that diligent application of the salve of Khan will enable significantly improved performance. The College Board's rhetoric implies that anyone will be able to study up to a 1600, which would—it seems to me—be both statistically impossible and undesirable from the perspective of the test's end users, the colleges who use scores to sort applicants. Or more strangely: If it proves possible for students to study their way to a high score, then the norms on which scores are based will become more and more stringent; the 1600 scorer of 2017 might be the 1350 scorer of 2024.)

There is of course the other kind of MOOC, the exploratory MOOC or xMOOC or whatever this month's terminology is, in which the online community engages in collective and collaborative inquiry and explication of a particular problem. These can be scaled down into courses with the look and feel of high school seminars of the junior and senior year ("The Coming of Age Novel in America," say, or "Studies in Genocide"), and rich and emotionally vibrant learning communities can be built around their themes.

Technology is going to make it easier to outsource instruction in ways that will bring more and more emotional depth to online and blended classrooms; this is a key and worthy objective of online schools operating in the independent school space, and I am confident that they, and in time perhaps other providers, have the depth of knowledge and understanding to do it properly.

But read, if you will, a sampling of the best narrative comments on elementary or middle school student work written by the most effective teachers at your school—assuming, of course, that you work in a school where teachers write narrative comments. Ask yourself a simple question: Could this comment have been written about a student working in an online environment?

The work of most independent school teachers—advising, coaching, looking after the fortunes of student clubs, and in some cases supervising dormitories (often referred to as "dorm parenting," to go right to the work's emotional content)—goes far, far beyond the basic function of classroom teaching and the simple transmission of knowledge, skills, and understandings that the popular mind has fixated on as "what teachers do." Much of this is true for teachers in any kind of setting, private, public, or charter.

What we forget is that the work of students in schools is equally complicated. Children in their pre-college years inhabit a bubbling 24/7 stew of developmental needs, opportunities, and challenges, and all of the other aspects of school life—the exploration of new ideas and ways of seeing the world, the sports, clubs, advisories, mealtimes, and above all friendships—are "growth experiences" in which the attentive, measured, perceptive mediation of adults is critically important. So important, in fact, that it is surely the essence of the "value proposition" that has families spending big bucks to obtain a certain brand of it for their private school children and certainly so important that it is the thing about their school days that most adults remember most vividly. This work, combined with the work that teachers do in "the affective domain," is the heart of school.

It would be a challenge for schools to outsource this heart, but I see plenty of signs of willingness to toss it out entirely. The focus of so much of the current public education reform movement on instruction and testing indicates to me that the heart of schools doesn't much matter to the reformers, and the wholesale closing of schools, dismissal of teachers, and expansion of class sizes works precisely against the really important heart work of providing settings for the mission-based, intentionally supported growth and development of children.

I've floated a new term of art on Twitter: *to umbridge*. Verb transitive: to tear the heart from a school or educational setting in the name of academic reform. Etymology: from Dolores Umbridge, the cold-hearted "reformer" who nearly ripped the life out of Hogwarts School in the *Harry Potter* novels of J.K. Rowling.

So let us not even think about outsourcing heart, and let us think even less about umbridging it. Let's remember that kids (and teachers, too) are human beings inhabiting vital communities and not just participants in instructional transactions with solely economic or vocational value.

I'm not so worried about the private sector here. The anti-heart forces trying to umbridge our public schools only make independent schools more attractive for those who can afford them. This is the sickest potential outcome of school "reform": that not only are the least affluent communities and the least affluent schools in danger of having heartful schools ripped away from them, but that in the end the children of socioeconomic "haves" might be further advantaged as emotional "haves," as well.

Not Your Father's School, March 10, 2014

10

PROFIT AND PROFITEERING IN EDUCATION

Lately I was gently (and privately) chided for expressing skepticism about the role of business enterprises—the people who sell us our computers, our textbooks, our desks, our apps, our standardized tests, our paper towels, and our trays of ravioli—in schools. Can't live without 'em. Gotta have 'em. We lionize the entrepreneurs who bring us our cool gadgets and apps, even as they amass billions, and we bend to the will of testing companies, for-profits that have spun testing enterprises off from lucrative textbook branches and gargantuan non-profits alike.

I know that schools need things and services. Buildings must be built, water and heat and light are essential, and we have to feed our students. Kids have to sit in chairs, and the technology on which we depend doesn't fall from the sky.

Many years ago I traveled to Washington, D. C., on some personal business. My grandparents had lived there, and so I remembered it as just another city, with more stirring architecture than most. But when I shopped for hotel rooms more or less downtown, I was shocked by the prices. Someone patiently explained to me that very few people visiting that part of the city pay their own way; some business or law firm or lobbying group is covering the cost, all expensible and deductible, and therefore rates are higher than what mere people would be willing to pay. "Regular" tourists stay out of town and take the Metro in to see the sights. Oh.

Experience has taught me that there are other such spots in the world. Geneva, Switzerland, for one. The institutional furniture industry, for another. Price out some of the really cool schoolroom furniture you see in "schools of the future," and you'll see that these schools, or school districts, are shelling out way more for these things than you or I would.

There's probably a term for this phenomenon, but I'll just call it "dis-economies of scale." Institutions buying in bulk and using other people's money (even if that is actually tuition revenue) wind up paying more for some items because their "consumers" are twice or thrice removed from the people who actually provide the dollars. Government agencies are notorious for this, and public schools are one of the largest arms of government. Independent schools, a relatively tiny market, wind up paying these artificially inflated prices because of the limited number of vendors, all of whom are accustomed to charging what I call government prices.

What's true for furniture is doubly true for textbooks. An experiment: See which would be a more luxe item to grace your coffee table, a nice art book from Amazon or a random French textbook; there are some cheaper textbooks, but the ones my kids toted around often out-cost colorful tomes on Matisse by a pretty penny. If you happen to pay for your kids' textbooks at an independent school or a college, do a price check. If you're an administrator signing off on billing these things, find out what parents are paying.

I'm not against publishers, of course, but I am pretty excited about teacher-created textbooks and assessments not just because they save money but because they can be expressly tailored to the learning objectives for a class. I know that kids have to sit somewhere, and I'll bet there are smaller suppliers who are making or could make neat stuff for less than six hundred bucks for a rolling chair-desk. Or maybe we could just ask our students to help us rearrange even some of the old-fashioned but movable furniture in our installed base.

Food service operators are a boon in all kinds of ways, I know, from solving HR issues to providing more nutritious meals; I think there actually are economies of scale in this realm.

I frown, however, when itchy investment money hovers directly over schools and school supplies, looking to snag big returns. I've written <u>elsewhere</u> of my opposition to for-profit schools in the public and charter realms; allowing business enterprises a profit margin on the backs of kids and taxpayers seems like bad public policy, especially when we have plenty of models of highly effective government-run schools. There has been huge growth in the for-profit standardized testing industry; every new scaling up of some testing regime—and many see the Common Core as culpable in this—seems to open the door for more profit-making. Educational technology has obviously benefited from the entrepreneurial spirit, fueled by venture capital, but scaling this into a sector dominated by online learning under a for-profit model just invites corner-cutting and lowest-common-denominator practices that are unlikely to serve every student well.

So I continue to reserve to myself the right to judge the difference between reasonable profit-making, businesses offering needed services and materiel for reasonable prices, and profiteering, extracting maximum revenue in exchange for goods and services in a model that puts investor returns over the good of students, schools, and taxpayers.

I am not anti-business, but much more am I pro-kid.

Not Your Father's School, December 17, 2013

11

INDEPENDENT SCHOOLS, DEMOCRACY, PLUTOCRACY, AND RESPONSIBILITY

A reader suggested offline that independent schools might not be a good thing in a democracy.

I know where he's coming from—the elitist tag sticks, a strange historical afterglow of the Gilded Age, when only the self-styled Right Sort of People seemed to send their children off to prep schools.

The issue isn't about democracy, but plutocracy. Plutocrats of a century ago were surely bloated, but if they did send their children to independent schools, it was a matter of choice— the heart of democracy. Eradicating this choice would strike me as being less about democracy than something far more problematic.

Of course nothing can excuse the virulently antidemocratic racism and anti-Semitism that characterized some independent schools into living memory. Some schools resisted these in the day, but many did not. This is a historical blot that cannot and will not be forgotten but that many schools have spent the past three decades and more trying to correct.

The earliest independent schools simply filled a gap that public schools did not yet exist to fill. Their pioneers tended to be dreamers and do-gooders: ministers, philosopher-teachers, and outright idealists like Bronson Alcott and Henry David Thoreau. At the beginning they charged fees because there weren't lots of free, open-enrollment alternatives.

Many will insist that independent schools were established to enshrine socioeconomic privilege. I won't argue that for a century or so they did largely that, although the origins of some of the most "exclusive" schools had, at least in their founders' eyes, a more idealistic raison d'etre: they were to educate to the children of the untethered wealthy— Robber Barons, some of them—who had neither the time, the inclination, nor perhaps even the values to raise boys and girls of intellectual and moral substance. Let there be boarding schools, they said, where these children could be taken in hand by adults with a firm sense of educational purpose and given a dose of discipline and some training in sportsmanship, serious academics, and the moral principles of muscular Christianity. In the absence of anything much better—private tutors while Mumsy traipses around Europe and Daddy busts aspiring unions?—this isn't too bad an impulse.

In Rudyard Kipling's *Captains Courageous* (1897) the spoiled son of a gazillionaire falls overboard from a transatlantic liner and is rescued by fishermen. A season aboard a fishing schooner makes a man of the lad, fitting him to eventually take over Daddy's empire as someone who had learned a thing or two about real life.

While you might not see the Gothic chapel of, say, Groton School (founded in 1884) as "real life," exactly, relatively Spartan living and enforced regimes of sports and study gave heirs-to-be a dose of *Captains Courageous*-like reality therapy. It's worth noting that a disproportion of early graduates of some these schools followed careers in public service (check out the "Notable alumni" list on Groton's *Wikipedia* page). They could afford to, you might say—and you'd be right—but some created the New Deal, which was arguably pretty good for democracy.

In the era of the One Percent, it's right to worry that independent schools might once again enshrine a separate elite; Fred Bartels has written eloquently about this in our industry's "trade magazine." Those who work in the schools know this, and thus such issues as affordability, socioeconomic diversity, and our "public purpose" are much on our lips and on our minds. There isn't an easy solution;

perhaps ironically, it's the established boarding schools that can offer the highest levels of need-based financial aid, and less affluent schools, despite some very egalitarian values and missions, are often in the weakest position to serve broad spectra of family incomes.

Our job as educators is to offer what those boarding school founders of the late nineteenth-century tried to: an education steeped in moral purpose as well as authentically connected to the requirements—social, cultural, and practical—of the "real world." We cannot, we know, simply surrender to the temptations of association with a new plutocracy.

Will our schools continue to serve the children of self-styled "elites"? Probably, to a greater degree than we like. We must acknowledge but never celebrate this, never embracing, endorsing, or excusing the concept of "elite," because our public purpose and our students' futures demand far, far better. Our challenge is to articulate and act on that demand.

"Independent Schools, Common Perspectives," *Education Week*, March 15, 2013

12

BIG MONEY, BIG GIFTS, AND INSTITUTIONAL VALUES

Over the weekend I found among my late father's books a 1956 paperback by William Richards titled *The Last Billionaire: Henry Ford*. I guess in the postwar prosperity that coupled reasonable tax rates with rapid economic growth in pretty much every sector, it must have looked as though bizarre income disparities and wealth gaps were things of the past. Oh, well. The folks at *Forbes* must be so relieved at how things have turned out.

So, speaking of vast wealth, the last couple of weeks have been pretty good for at least a couple of fundraisers.

Stanford has wrapped up a six-billion-dollar capital campaign just as Harvard was proclaiming its own, for six-and-a-half. And on September 30 the president of Yale announced a single $250-million-dollar gift from an alum, a sum that Yale plans to use toward the building of a couple of new residential colleges, thus expanding undergraduate enrollment by about 15%, a big increase but probably not one that will make a dent in Yale's already rarefied admission numbers. A quarter of a billion dollars is a serious gift, and I imagine there was some dancing in the offices of Yale's senior administration.

Then last week I heard from Mercersburg Academy in Pennsylvania that it had received a $107 million gift from an alum, an amount that edges out of the all-time Number Two spot a hundred-million-dollar gift made by Walter Annenberg to his alma mater, The Peddie School, twenty years ago. Arguably inflation makes the Annenberg gift larger in practice, but at that level I don't think there's much point in quibbling.

Private education in this country, college or K–12, often gets a bad rap as being elitist and all about money. No child of wealth on TV or in the movies can avoid going to a school where everyone wears insignia'd blazers and where the boys are named Chad and the girls Muffy. There they flounce about amid ridiculous luxury and privilege, one-upping one another in snobbery and acquisitiveness. High-profile gifts of nine digits don't exactly help dispel the image, as inaccurate as it is for so many private colleges—the majority of whom have to hustle hard for students and donations—and independent schools.

An October 7 <u>op-ed by student Scott Stern in the *Yale Daily News*</u> raises another, larger issue: What is the influence of Big Money on education, even at a place like Yale, where even a giant gift represents only a relative drop in a $20.8 billion endowment bucket? Put more edgily, don't big gifts tend to come with agendas and expectations, even if the expectations are carefully masked by words of openness and pure intention?

We've got a whole lot of billionaires in this country, and more than a few of them throw their money at various charitable causes at levels that I would be churlish to characterize as anything other than extra generous, although I'm guessing most could double their giving levels and still manage to live fairly comfortably. Some of them make no bones about having an agenda behind their giving; Bill and Melinda Gates, for example, have an idea about education and are committed to funding that idea.

Skepticism along the lines expressed by Yale's Stern is nothing new, and it is part of a proud tradition in educational funding discussions that goes back at least to the days of the "divest in South Africa" controversies on college campuses in the 80s and protests against the military-industrial complex and even the Free Speech Movement on some campuses in the 1960s. We are aware in our society that money talks, and we're equally aware (well, all of us but the Supremes in the majority on Citizens United) that the trumpetings of money can stifle the voices of those who don't have it. There's also a modern practice of looking at the source of long-ago wealth on which contemporary institutions are based—such as the slaveholders and robber barons whose money formed the kernel of more than a few currently fat college endowments.

I don't know whether there's a secret agenda behind the Yale or Mercersburg gifts, or whether the moneys given were earned in ways that would pass everyone's righteousness test. Being generally pleased at the idea that these gifts are headed toward educational institutions I respect, I have to check myself. I was pretty thrilled at the formation of the Gates Foundation, too, but I am less pleased by some of its direction today, and what Diane Ravitch calls the "Billionaire Boys' Club" is surely not pushing public education toward places I'm entirely pleased with. I have my own agenda, of course, and maybe it's fortunate that I don't have billions with which to fund it. Big money and the spending thereof seem to make people weird.

A giant gift, in my humble opinion, should spur reflection on the part of the recipient, a time to take stock of the institutional values that such a gift should be, above all things, meant to sustain or promote. It's a time for institutions, even ones as vast and varied as Yale, to hold just a bit more tightly to their missions and fundamental values—the ones that are about people and society, maybe even ones that are a mite on the spiritual side, at least enough to remind us that unto whomsoever much is given, of them shall be much required.

This is an old sentiment, but not, I think, an obsolete one, and I like to believe that it still means something to those at Yale and Mercersburg and dozens of other places on whom the philanthropic deities have been smiling of late.

"Independent Schools, Common Perspectives," *Education Week*, October 15, 2013

13

WHEN NONPROFITS GO CORPORATE: CAUTIONARY TALES

I have written before about <u>kids and the great outdoors</u>—nature-deficit disorder, the suburbanization of the country day school, and the de-naturing of the curriculum. Maybe it's the summer, seeing the word "July" on the calendar. I look forward to water views and leafy shade in a spot that's cool-ish and devoid of distractions. I can write, and reflect, in either order.

Years ago my outdoor summers were spent working in residential "youth camps." I was lucky enough to find work over the years at a series of "agency" camps, working my way up from lowest person in the kitchen to, in time, camp director, like someone in Gilbert & Sullivan. Latterly I shuffled back down the ladder of success, ending my camp career as a humble, sunburned boat driver. The camps were all run by the regional subdivisions of large non-profit organizations; in fact, all but one (a YWCA camp) were run by the Girl Scouts.

My first gig was at a sailing camp on a New England resort island. Where presidents have since spent zillions of our tax dollars to vacation, I lived in a tent and was paid to slice tomatoes, keep the plumbing working, and haul trash around in a pick-up truck. It was, for everyone there, an idyll.

In time, however, something happened. The body that owned the camp was absorbed in a merger of multiple Girl Scout councils, and business-minded council executives replaced the very camp-y and program-focused folks who had run the smaller councils. They had discovered the phrase "economies of scale." The many camps (smallish and beloved of their campers over decades) that had comprised the smaller councils became a very few camps, larger and

46

under centralized operation that no doubt lowered the cost of toilet paper and canned goods. Soon my island camp was on the auction block; the new council leadership had visions of sixteen island acres generating a couple of million 1982 dollars—a big chunk of change.

There was weeping, wailing, threats of lawsuits, and lots of anger, including mine. In the end, ironically, various environmental and zoning restrictions meant that only the town was really able to buy the property, for a federally-subsidized song. It's now a town park, happily available for public use and the site of a community sailing program that probably does as much to instill a love of sailing in kids as the old camp once did.

Thirty years later, de-accessioning camps has become a hallmark of the Girl Scout movement nationally. Having apparently invested its pension funds poorly (one wonders in what? buggy whip futures?), the national organization and its local councils—having completed a dizzying spate of mergers—are holding a kind of national fire sale of camps. The issue has been all over the news, and in my household, where five of our own past Girl Scout camps and, for good measure that YWCA camp, have been sold or are for sale, we're pretty unhappy. Better organized and perhaps more reflexively litigious than we were thirty years ago, camp-sale opponents have launched any number of lawsuits and have of course set up Facebook pages and other sites to keep the war drums beating.

The relevance here, in case you were wondering, is double:

First, the closed camps represent thousands of empty bunks and dining hall chairs, thousands of opportunities lost for kids to spend time in the out-of-doors. The Scouts claim that kids aren't interested in camping so much these days, but in part that's because the organization has de-emphasized camping programs in its quest for some new and thus far elusive magic bullet to interest girls in Scouting. Plenty

47

of private camps—even non-profit, non-Scout camps—are doing just fine.

Second, there's a fascination in many quarters of the educational world—often the quarters that aren't parts of school campuses but rather in think tanks, political strategy sessions, and sometimes the heads of corporate-minded independent school trustees—with business-think. The lesson here is clear: economies of scale seduced the former Patriots' Trail Girl Scout Council in 1982 and clearly grabbed the imagination of Girl Scouts USA as it encouraged the larger wave of mergers that began in the 1990s; the mergers, of course, resulted in a great spate of camp closings in their own right. And when the organization found itself short on pension funds, how quick it was to find a simple solution: peddle the camps. (Of course, even cookie sale proceeds are also being used indirectly to offset pension losses.) The new methods and aims turned out to be antithetical to and destructive of the fundamental aims of the organization.

Maybe the Girl Scouts and the YWCA will find that magic bullet, some new way to engage girls by the hundreds of thousands and bring their membership back to the levels of yore; that'd be great, and as an educator I would stand up and applaud. But in the meantime, I've lived through, and paid in memories for, what happens when the corporate mindset takes over an enterprise—Scouting and the camp movement, in my case—whose mission and goals are about children's learning and well-being, when business-bedazzled "reformers" perform their special, misguided magic.

"Independent Schools, Common Perspectives," *Education Week*, July 3, 2013

14

READING FOR A WEIRD WINTER: MCLUHAN, MARKETWORLD, AND ADOLESCENCE

If there is anything about the winter of 2018–19 that hasn't been pretty strange somewhere, I haven't heard about it—and I mean everything from weather to governance. Sometimes I just need to curl up with a good book, and lately I have found a few.

It's been four decades and change since I last picked up Marshall McLuhan's *The Medium is the Massage* (with its utterly forgotten subtitle, "An Inventory of Effects"), and as social media sinks us ever more deeply into the Mass Age, a young colleague suggested I give the book another shot. And, boy, am I glad I did.

McLuhan was doing a lot of crazy predicting in 1967, and a bunch of those have come true. In particular his view of where the Electronic Age was taking education has turned out to be spot-on. Try this: "The classroom is now in a vital struggle for survival with the immensely persuasive 'outside' world created by new information media." McLuhan's cry for making education relevant is equally clear: "The young today want roles—R.O.L.E.S. That is, total involvement." Between pages 100 and 101 of the newish <u>Gingko Press edition</u>, McLuhan lays out the case for rejecting one-right-answer schooling as compellingly as any guru of 2019. Read (or re-read) this book.

My head is spinning and my heart occasionally pounding as I take in *<u>Winners Take All by Anand Giridharadas</u>*. I bounce from profound guilt at the industry in which I spent my institutional career to anger at the charade that "conscious capitalists" and "social entrepreneurs" have been pulling to downright embarrassment at having been duped by a TED

Talk here or an article in *Fast Company* there. Giridharadas's thesis is that economic elites have arrogated to themselves the role of social saviors even as many their solutions—think some of the trumpeting from Davos, oopsies from the Clinton Foundation, and the hype around Airbnb—exacerbate profound and growing economic and social inequality. He calls this perspective "MarketWorld," and in independent schools we have become way too familiar with arguments—usually advanced by those with the economic power to prevail—that schools need to be "run like businesses" instead of mission-driven crucibles of the human spirit. While not explicitly a critique of education or independent schools in particular, Giridharadas's argument implicitly takes independent schools to task not only for their very existence as evidence of privilege but especially with regard to "community service" and other programs—including aspects of many that fall under the trendy rubrics of entrepreneurship and "innovation"—that celebrate the idea of "doing well by doing good."

(As in, my friends, those service hours and trips to underresourced places that serve as evidence of compassion on college applications. Not that these don't represent compassion and awakening understanding truly and deeply for many, many students, but rather in the ways we encourage and even celebrate their wielding as instruments of personal aggrandizement in our résumé-obsessed world.)

But it's all for the kids, and on that front <u>Dana Czapnik's novel *The Falconer*</u> (no relation to a work of the same name by our friend Grant Lichtman) stands out. The *New York Times* review that compelled me to buy *The Falconer* made comparisons to J. D. Salinger, and the book delivers. Protagonist Lucy Adler is a senior, Class of 1994, at a New York City independent school, and being Lucy is incredibly complicated. Her explorations of herself, feminism, herself, friendship, herself, class divisions, herself, racism, and what it means to be a young woman whose nature, proclivities, and propensities focus on desires and interests outside the norms of the world she must navigate are extraordinary. As an aging white guy reading this book, I was in constant amazement. I probably taught a few Lucy Adlers in that very same era, and I felt profoundly sad and occasionally embarrassed as this Lucy's perspective unfolded in both urgent and poignant detail. As is too usual in novels involving independent schools, adults, including well-intended teachers, come off as largely disengaged and ineffectual.

(*The Falconer* is also a kind of love letter to the Big Apple that reminds me, strangely but happily, of Madeleine L'Engle's young adult novel _The Young Unicorns_, which once inspired me to take a field trip. Its setting is also nearly contemporaneous with Whit Stillman's New York City films _Metropolitan_ and _The Last Days of Disco_, with their own bitter prep school echoes.)

I notice that two out of three of these books prompt shame. Perhaps this is because I am embarrassed so often these days by the system we live in, by the leaders we have, and by my reflections on my own sins of omission. I can plead ignorance—after all, we are all works in progress from cradle to grave—and I can plead economic and political impotence. But we all have a great deal of work to do in order to fix this world, and for most of us that work begins by figuring out how and where we can actually help. I working on it.

McLuhan reminds us how we are letting technology separate learning from life. Giridharadas reminds us how the chasms between the wealthy and even the middle-class, much less "the poor," separate us as human beings in a time when real and selfless collaboration and cooperation are more needed than ever. Czapnik shows how separating one part of the self from another through artificial social and economic distinctions adds to the already enormous burdens of growing up (though her Lucy does so, most assuredly).

51

Can we please, please, as educators and humans, find ways to build a world of holistic education and common purpose that allows our children to be fully and authentically themselves?

Not Your Father's School, February 18, 2019

A POSITIVE SOCIAL GOOD? INDEPENDENT SCHOOLS' OBLIGATIONS TO THE SOCIETY THAT PRIVILEGES THEM

The section title and the essays speak for themselves here. They're just my sometimes flailing attempts to frame and respond to some rather big questions:

What, in the end, are independent schools good for?

What efforts and initiatives might independent schools take to see and acknowledge their historical position and privileges in ways that could establish them as a more useful and ethical presence on the educational landscape?

Why do independent schools continue to exist?

What if independent schools didn't exist?

15

IF INDEPENDENT SCHOOLS HAD TO GO AWAY: A THOUGHT EXPERIMENT

The little voices inside my Twitter feed calling for the end of independent schools as a solution to our nation's "1% Problem" won't go away. So I'm going to try a little exercise to see where that point of view could lead.

I'm assuming that the voices' ideal would be a government seizure of all 1400 independent schools, with subsequent closures, reallocation of cash and real assets, and (I guess) the forced repatriation of their thousands of tuition-paying international students. (Lest we forget, private schools, like higher education, are one sector in which the "balance of trade" is favorable to the United States.)

But this scenario is unlikely, at least since the failure of the fictional coup d'état in *Seven Days in May* back in 1964.

More likely, there would be some gradual mandated return of independent schools and their students to the public domain. One way to accomplish this would be for independent schools, with their individual cultures and missions, to "charterize." What might this look like?

Let's imagine that the board of trustees at St. Basalt's School (henceforth StBS), a Massachusetts day/boarding school serving grades 6 through 12, is given the mandate to turn StBS into a charter school.

First, StBS would need to apply for a charter. Before doing so, it might be prudent for the board to split the school into two functions: one, the school as an educational enterprise, and two, a holding company that would own the campus, buildings, and equipment. Assuming the charter were granted, StBS (the school) could make arrangements with StBS (the real estate company) to purchase or lease the campus, solving what is typically a major problem for new charter schools. It should be noted that, although independent schools are subject to building codes and other such regulations, as a state-chartered entity StBS Charter would probably encounter new bureaucratic layers to navigate.

StBS would be allowed to admit as many students as permitted in its charter. By law, enrollment would be open but absolutely limited to state residents—no tuition-paying out-of-staters. As revenue, each student would bring his or her district's Per Pupil Expenditure, which might vary, one from another, by as much as ten percent.

The good news is that StBS would be permitted to hold onto its endowment and to continue fund-raising, thus enabling it to pad out the per-pupil district payments toward extra or enhanced services—smaller classes, personalized advising, better-funded clubs and activities. Other activities or services could be subject to auxiliary service charges, even boarding—although the school could not establish quotas or limits on day enrollment versus boarding, making the budgeting of a boarding program something of a challenge. And remember, no out-of-state or international students.

StBS teachers, with classes now representing the full range of randomness in the admission lottery pool, would need to be prepared to teach a wider range, and so the StBS professional development program would need to expand. Lost in the randomness, perhaps, would be any active commitment that StBS had previously made to increasing particular kinds of student diversity. Lost, too, would be any heritage or continuity in certain programs, like athletics or performing arts.

Oh, and there's one more thing: StBS students would now be subject to state testing requirements. For those who believe such tests are The Great Equalizer, *Bam! Problem solved!* However, I suspect that those who love not independent schools love widespread testing even less.

Well, here is one way to actually imagine the demise of independent schools and the redistribution of access and programs (to an extent, anyhow) for the common good. It certainly isn't simple, and I'm not sure that I see a clear benefit. StBS, for example, could use its inherited assets (endowment, campus, equipment) to become a kind of "Cadillac" charter program, although open enrollment would do nothing more than make it more desirable as a lottery ticket, a super-er Superman for whom to wait. But it could also, if it chose, continue to be a "lab school" for its own mission and for any particular approaches to teaching and learning on which it had been working. Yet another "but," though: StBS would also lose its culture as a national or international community. All told, the new StBS Charter School would probably be more democratic, at least with respect to admissions. I'd even go so far as to stipulate that the STBS faculty could rise to the occasion of teaching a more academically and cognitively diverse student body.

What this scenario would not achieve is level-funding of all schools or guaranteed across-the-spectrum program equity, both useful goals for American education but which aren't achieved by any model we've yet concocted; they fly in the face of our tendency to mistrust "leveling" efforts when they affect ourselves, not just other people. Anyhow, lamentably that train has long since left the station.

I undertook this experiment with some trepidation, but it seemed worthwhile to try to play out the independent school skeptics' position, just to see where it might lead. I can't say that I'm sold on the idea. I still believe there are plenty of ways that St. Basalt's School and its kin can and do serve the public good. The temptations of elitism can be avoided, I still believe, and public purpose affirmed in words and, more significantly, in deeds.

I've said it before: Independent schools can surely commit to being, not part of the 1% Problem, but important ingredients of a 99% solution.

(I must add here my emphatic and eternal gratitude to Greg Orpen, principal of the high school at <u>Innovation Academy Charter School</u> in Tyngsboro, Massachusetts, who provided me with general pointers on Massachusetts charter school law and listened to my slightly crazed questions with admirable patience.)

"Independent Schools, Common Perspectives," *Education Week*, July 17, 2013

16

TRUTH AND RECONCILIATION: A CHALLENGE TO SCHOOLS

"I (we) wish to acknowledge this land on which the University of Toronto operates. For thousands of years it has been the traditional land of the Huron-Wendat, the Seneca, and most recently, the Mississaugas of the Credit River. Today, this meeting place is still the home to many Indigenous people from across Turtle Island and we are grateful to have the opportunity to work on this land."

This invocation, known officially as the "Statement of Acknowledgement of Traditional Land" (the Canadian spelling is the University of Toronto's), begins every official function at the university. Developed "in consultation with First Nations House and its Elders Circle, some scholars in the field, and senior University officials," the statement grows out of truth and reconciliation efforts across Canada, and it is apparently only one example of a growing genre.

I've occasionally written about the heritage issues that might trouble the sleep of many independent schools. Creatures of their times and places, schools have not been immune to the influences of racism, sexism, and religious prejudice that shaped and continue to pollute North American society. But few schools have taken a look at the very land on which they sit—land whose history prior to European colonization is sometimes obscure but almost never unknowable.

As any school that has found itself on the losing end of an eminent domain decision knows, land "ownership" is never pure and seldom simple; multiple jurisdictions (village, town, county, state, nation) have potential legal claims, for example, upon the land where sits the house that I like to think that I own. But before there were Norfolk County and the Commonwealth of Massachusetts, there were millennia of native peoples with their own complex social, cultural, and political histories, and being reminded of this enriches my appreciation for those histories. It also deepens my uncomfortable understanding of the ways in which these lands became owned by white European settlers and strengthens my desire and will not to be part of oppression in my own time.

It happens that one of my kids is working on a doctorate at Toronto, focusing on literatures of oppressed and underrepresented cultures, largely in diaspora. He told me about the university's statement during a conversation about "Pocahontas deniers"—an apparently real slice of our population who apparently don't believe or will not acknowledge that Native Americans ever existed, or even that indigenous people exist in North America today. I want to deny these deniers, but apparently they are out there, like so many other deniers of one sort or another, haughty and increasingly dangerous in their willful ignorance.

So why don't all our institutions have their own statements of acknowledgment of "Traditional Land"? You might call such a notion fussily politically correct, but schools, at least, have a purpose to be purveyors of truth, especially about themselves. What good might come of making the effort to trace the past possessors and users of the land before it became the farm or estate or other disused institution where now lies your school? What good might there be in exploring and promoting an understanding of "Turtle Island" as a construct that predates (and interrogates in a powerful way) "manifest destiny"?

What good might come of creating a course or a club or a committee of students who might reach out to build connections with the contemporary indigenous neighbors and cultural bodies that exist everywhere in North America?

What benefit might there be in refuting the deniers and those who believe or have been taught, as I sort of was more than a half-century ago, that Native Peoples mostly bowed off history's stage at roughly the beginning of the 20th century—casino gambling, Western movies, and photogenic rituals notwithstanding?

There are readers who will say this seems like a small and trivial point to be making against the backdrop of all the work we have to do as educators. But this concept aligns not just with general educational ideals about light and truth but also aligns quite specifically with, say, the <u>Principles of Independent Curriculum</u>: "Congruent with the mission and values of the school;" "High intellectual and ethical standards;" and "Inclusive and just." It even requires the creation of understood connections between "history" and the real lives and real school work and play spaces of students and teachers—the New Relevance, of which <u>I have written elsewhere</u>, made manifest.

As colleges struggle publicly and privately with legacies of slavery and racism, a great many independent schools these days are facing their own obligation to "truth and reconciliation" around past issues of abuse. Truth will out, it seems, so why not look at every aspect of one's history that might need some explaining and some reconciliation?

I believe that sooner or later, like colleges, schools are going to have to face even more troubling aspects of their own histories. We have shied away so far, perhaps in the belief that these things are not for children, but it strikes me that developing a statement around the very land a school occupies might be a good place to start. It's a way to send a message that we are really prepared to talk about—and do something about—the hard stuff.

So come on, schools! Step up to the plate of truth and reconciliation. If we have anything to be thankful for in 2019, it is the persistence of truth, and our task as educators is to be its champion, even when it hurts.

The Independent Curriculum Blog, November 26, 2019; updated from *Not Your Father's School,* July 12, 2017

17

INDEPENDENT SCHOOL RESPONSIBILITIES: 'TEST KITCHENS' AND SUSTAINING A NATION

The other day the *New York Times* ran <u>a long-ish piece</u> on the sometimes troubled relationship between charter and traditional public schools. This is a hot-button issue in all kinds of ways, but the article focused on what constitutional scholars might call original intent: the idea that the charter school movement began largely in the spirit of "let a hundred flowers bloom"—to provide, in the rather apt phrase of the *Times*, a "test kitchen" for new educational and pedagogical practices that would, if found to be successful, become regular new items on public school menus.

Like plenty of other educators, twenty years ago I found the charter idea intriguing, provocative, even downright excellent—and slightly familiar. In the independent school community, a pretty wide range of doing things has been part of our culture for a century or more, sometimes based on deep intent and at others based on some founder or other leader's strongly held idiosyncratic notions about how this or that educational work might best be done. Sometimes, it is true, the weight of mere tradition has come to be the determinant of a school's destiny, but dig into the history of most independent schools and you are likely to find something pedagogically interesting and unique in its founding impulses.

Unlike the origin of charter schools, in the independent school world there doesn't ever seem to have been anything like an expectation of "idea flow" back toward the public sector. In general, independent schools have tended to represent a kind of brain drain in which both teachers and students either have never participated in or in some way have disappeared from public education. Along with this drain there has been, let's face it, an inevitable diminution in the interest of these educators and their students' families in the overall state of their communities' public schools. (Of course a handful of these people have lately reappeared in the public sector as advocates for corporate-style reforms that don't much reflect their independent school experiences, but that is a subject for another day.)

But in independent schools, some interesting things have been going on, some for a very long time and others brand new. Independent schools have always been free to be their very own test kitchens, and they have cooked up some pretty savory and successful recipes for their own consumption, although there has been a recent trend toward a bit more intra-sector sharing. Keeping in mind that these schools do serve a fairly wide range of students (although generally less wide than most public systems when taken school by school) and operate with a broad range of missions (although preparation for secondary education and college tend to be at the center of their work), we would expect to find a rich variety of educational practices in all areas: pedagogy, curriculum and assessment, "character education," program design, and even professional development.

I've called here and elsewhere for more inter-sector dialogue, because despite my personal career path, I am a believer in the traditional model of public education. I've even been a part of a tiny, nascent effort to build this dialogue, the #PubPriBridge, along with my sometime offerings in this space. It's a core belief for me that independent school educators have much to learn from our public school counterparts, and I always search for signs of real balance and reciprocity whenever I hear about independent school–public school "partnerships." The echoes of noblesse-oblige I still occasionally hear give me hives.

But in matters of teaching and learning, independent schools may have real things to share. If independent schools are test kitchens, do they (we) have an obligation to put our successful practices out there, in the spirit of the original charter idea, for the rest of the educational world to consider and perhaps incorporate? If the original charter model was rather independent school-like—building-level governance, relatively regulation-free—couldn't it even be argued that the educational reformers behind the first charters missed a bet? Why not have started by putting some responsibilities on existing "test kitchens," a thousand and more independent schools, to share what they know?

I've been saying this in other ways for a while, but the charter analogy and the test kitchen metaphor have further clarified for me the idea that independent schools might have an actual responsibility to share what we know as a kind of quid pro quo for our other liberties. Independent school students and their families may have absented themselves from public schools, but there is no reason that our practices need to do so. In return for tax-exemptions and public acquiescence to our relatively unregulated existence, why not give back by sharing what we know best: our own experiences related to teaching and learning?

Sharing what we know about educational practice does not and should not, of course, excuse independent schools and their people from listening to and otherwise engaging with public school educators as peers. An independent school-led professional development program for public school educators (and there are a few of these around the country, good and earnest ones that can be models for the kind of sharing I'm talking about) cannot be exclusively a one-way presentation but indeed must be an authentic conversation among equals—just the kind of conversation most independent school educators happily discover themselves to be in on those rare occasions when teachers from both sectors find themselves learning together in a room.

Independent school test kitchens, to stretch this metaphor to its final millimeter, have been cranking out a variety of good ideas for a while; it's time we figured out how to add what we know to the urgent task of nourishing and sustaining a whole nation of learners and schools.

"Independent Schools, Common Perspectives," *Education Week*, May 13, 2014

18

THE RIGHT QUESTION FROM INDEPENDENT SCHOOLS

The other day John Chubb, president of the National Association of Independent Schools, a previous interviewee here and here, and once the object of some gentle prodding from this quarter, blogged about a visit he and NAIS vice-president for government and community relations Jefferson Burnett recently made to meet with Education Secretary Arne Duncan.

Apparently cabinet secretaries are accustomed to importunate callers; by Chubb's account, the meeting started with Duncan's people more or less asking, "So, what do you guys want?"

I suppose there's still plenty that the independent school industry could ask for. But NAIS schools operate largely outside of federal educational regulation and benefit from tax laws that support charitable giving to educational non-profits (which all NAIS member schools are and must be), so any request at the cabinet level beyond a continuation of these privileges might smack of excess.

The NAIS delegation, however, turned the tables on Duncan and responded with a paraphrase of JFK's famous line regarding what citizens can do for our country: "We're here to ask what we can do for you."

Here and there in this blog I've suggested that there are positive goods that independent schools might offer up as contributions to the national conversation on and maybe even the direction of educational practice. We've been busy developing new approaches to curriculum and assessment while many public schools have been hugely distracted by

No Child Left Behind-inspired standardized testing regimes. We've been developing our own academic standards, mostly at the school level, that seem to satisfy colleges and universities without need for a common core. Our teachers are generally pretty happy and our students largely engaged. Research from The Association of Boarding Schools, another group of independent schools, suggests that by and large its member schools, against stereotype, are actually more racially and culturally diverse, on a school-by-school basis, than many public schools, which have been settling back into *de facto* segregation as communities and neighborhoods stratify as a manifestation of the increasing socioeconomic stratification of which President Obama recently spoke.

We also have resources that are being deployed to support professional and community development in the public sector. Parts of many of our campuses are regularly used as community resources. We know there's more we can offer, and groups like the National Network of Schools in Partnership are helping schools find ways to offer it.

So what Chubb & Company had to say to Secretary Duncan was definitely the right question. "What can we do to help?" is exactly what the independent school sector should be asking, and I am pleased and even proud that our industry chiefs have asked it.

I wasn't quite as impressed by the Secretary's reported wish list; there is some good stuff, like "help with education technology" and "blended learning models that provide documented academic benefits," but at the same time there seems to be an unsurprising but tiresome focus on the business side. "They want to leverage online and other technology businesses. They are looking for a group of schools that might agree on the specifications of a comprehensive platform for the full range of school technologies and lure firms to develop to that platform—increasing quality and reducing price." I'm suspicious enough of this kind of talk to see in such ambitions the specter of corporatization and perhaps even privatization.

The Secretary is also interested in boarding schools as models for "affective" education for students "in the most disadvantaged circumstances." There are a handful of great models here—<u>Milton Hershey School</u>, <u>Christina Seix Academy</u>—but I'd hate to see us as a nation try to scale these up in ways that don't, like Seix Academy, engage families and communities as part of their model. We've already tried separating disadvantaged children from their communities in failed experiments we call "<u>Native American boarding schools</u>," "reform schools," and "prisons."

But I was happy to read that Chubb's post ends with some conversation with Duncan about things that independent schools do well and that, properly resourced, could scale well—namely, offering programs and pedagogical models that truly engage students. This is a centerpiece of many independent school programs, and schools with a wide range of missions successfully engage students with an equally great range of backgrounds, capacities, and interests.

Some independent school folks may worry that an NAIS exec who offers the D of E a helping hand might not be sufficiently tending his own shop, but I think that Dr. Chubb's offer contains opportunities for schools not only to dig in and do our work even more effectively but also, as a side benefit, to strengthen our industry's position in the national mind and even in the marketplace—just what NAIS needs.

Supporting the public sector ought to be an important industry goal in whatever ways we can accomplish it; as Americans we've got the future of millions of kids besides those in our own schools to worry about. By doing well by them, by asking what we can do for our country and then doing it, we'll be okay.

And, by the way, I tip my hat to John Chubb.

"Independent Schools, Common Perspectives," *Education Week*, December 9, 2013

19

ANOTHER INVISIBLE KNAPSACK: INDEPENDENT SCHOOL PRIVILEGE (MY TAKE)

PREFACE 1, with a slightly red face: Little did I know (or remember) when I wrote this last night that Guybe Slangen, the organizer of the Private Schools with Public Purpose Conference referenced below, had put this very same concept into words in <u>a piece for</u> Independent School <u>magazine</u> in 2009. I strongly urge readers to have a look at Guybe's writing, which prefigures what I have written below and adds a great deal, I think, to the case for unpacking this knapsack.

PREFACE 2: This post is made in awed homage to the great Peggy McIntosh, whose essay "<u>White Privilege: Unpacking the Invisible Knapsack</u>" has had a lasting influence on the dialogue on race and justice in schools and society since it exploded into our collective consciousness in 1989.

The evolution of my thinking on independent schools and their role in the larger educational community took a turn the other day as I was preparing to present with my #PubPriBridge colleagues Chris Thinnes and Laura Robertson, along with our new friend Brad Weaver, at the recent <u>Private Schools with Public Purpose Conference</u> in San Francisco.

In my part of the presentation, which I delivered as a talking head via Skype, I asked session participants to consider the nature and the history of independent schools' rather charmed status on the outside of most educational regulation and beyond the reach of much local and national tax policy. In passing, I likened this to white privilege: largely unearned (more on this below) and full of free passes and hidden and not-so-hidden advantages.

In Peggy McIntosh's famous essay, she lists a number of ways in which the unearned privilege of whiteness conveys immunity from real troubles and even casual discordance. (Others have used the trope to create analogous lists of the privileges of heterosexuality and other socially privileged statuses.)

So, as derivative (but I hope not tired) as the concept might be, here are some of the ways in which independent schools are privileged in the educational community:

Independent schools are free to determine their own missions and develop their own values and visions.

Independent schools can decide to raise money when they wish to, without worrying about local approval or political attitudes on property tax hikes or bond issues.

Independent schools can hire who they want to, regardless of special licensure or certification.

Independent schools can promote whom they want to, regardless of administrative or other special licensure or certification.

Independent schools' governing bodies are not determined by general elections but by self-perpetuating groups of like-minded individuals.

Independent schools are free to determine their own criteria for student admission, honoring only the most basic tenets of certain broad Federal regulations such as IDEA, the ADA, and various civil rights laws.

Independent schools are free to determine their own criteria for student retention and promotion, within the broadest of Federal guidelines.

Independent schools are free to determine their own criteria for teacher retention and assignment, within the broadest of Federal guidelines.

Independent schools are free to determine exactly how much money they wish to spend on educating each student and how much they charge each family, subject only to their own interpretation of regional and local market forces.

Independent schools are free to teach what they wish, in the manner they wish, subject only to state guidelines and local regulations that do not tend to impinge heavily on curriculum and assessment.

Independent schools may, subject to compliance with state guidelines, issue their own bonds through state-sponsored authorities on terms that are favorable rates for investors.

Independent schools may seek and expect to receive donations, large and small, from their supporters, unimpeded by regulation and with their donors given incentive by tax relief.

Independent schools students may, subject only to broad state or regional guidelines, participate in athletic competitions and other extracurricular activities based only on guidelines or criteria for participation set by the schools themselves.

With rare exceptions, independent schools students may learn and have their learning assessed outside of sometimes onerous state-sponsored regimes of regular, mandated standardized testing; their teachers are relieved of the obligation to prepare students for such tests and of the possibility of having their performance being evaluated by student results on such testing.

Independent schools can be assured that their students will be disproportionately represented in the admitted pools of the nation's most selective and prestigious colleges and universities. (An instance of privilege granted by custom and not by policy.)

Independent schools can assume that they have a place of primacy in local and regional (and in rare cases, national) conversations about educational prestige. (Another instance of privilege granted by custom and not by policy.)

Privileges are, however, what one makes of them, and educators' discussions around race and sexual orientation (for example) demonstrate that the effects of unconscious privilege can be mitigated by recognition and more importantly by dialogue and even training in which the ears of the privileged are attuned to bias and inequity—the assumption is that people in general recognize the benefits of a society in which the unearned advantage of a few has been neutralized in favor of true merit.

What would a similar dialogue look like that involved schools and the recognition of their privileges, many of which are etymologically literal "private laws"? How can the pernicious effects of privilege be mitigated when so many of independent schools' advantages are established by legislation and official regulation rather than simply by custom? If independent schools can't shake off the effects of unearned privilege simply by being wise and informed, as in relation to racial bias and homophobia, what can we do? If the authorities insist on reinforcing our advantage, do we really even need to see this as a problem?

Sure, on a superficial plane this privilege is hardly a problem for schools. But we live in an age when we are eagerly proclaiming our "public purpose" and where "social justice" and "civic engagement" are on the tips of many, many institutional tongues. Ought we then to at least recognize that we have such privilege? Don't we need to acknowledge that in our efforts to express our public purpose, to become places of justice, and to engage civically, we need at least to consider the ways in which the field on which we and our students are playing is not even close to level?

And to be sure, this un-levelness is a clear impediment to our efforts to engage, as I often urge independent schools and their people to do, in symmetrical conversations about teaching and learning with our counterparts in other sectors. We need to understand not only the nature of our privileges but also their effects—and beyond that, the way in which these effects can warp our own perspectives, with the best will in the world, on issues of common concern to all educators. We have to take responsibility for that which has been thrust upon us by lawmakers and regulators, not to reject it (which we can't really do) but to acknowledge that it affects our perspective and must force us—if we really want to engage with our counterparts and express our "public purpose"—to consider even more carefully the perspectives of others.

Independent schools do good work, and it's probable that some of this good work is in fact a product of the freedoms that we are afforded. But in the just society that we say we want, every school should be able to do good work and every student, in every school, should be its beneficiary.

If there are advantages to the ways in which we are allowed to operate, we should be seeking these for every school and actively leading the efforts to achieve this goal. If there are things to which our privileges blind us, we ought to be seeking ways to see these more clearly.

But just to continue on, blissfully taking advantage of our relative institutional autonomy without seeing this as carrying a certain responsibility to even things out in our relations with society as whole—to be a "social good"—is to live in exactly that place of ignorance that as educators we deplore when we encounter it as privileged bias in our students, our colleagues, or in ourselves.

Gain perspective, we say; understand how privilege distorts and limits your view of the world and of others. Good advice to students, and extremely good advice to ourselves.

Not Your Father's School, March 15, 2015

20

PARTNERSHIP, COMMUNITY-STYLE: SCHOOLS IN THEIR PROPER PLACE

Sometimes at conferences I find my mind wandering, heading off into little neural riffs and speculations triggered by something I'm listening to. Since there's probably not going to be a quiz on the presentation, I guess this is allowed. Quite possibly this should be the point of being there in the first place.

Yesterday morning I was at the 2014 National Association of Independent Schools annual conference, where I sat in on a session moderated by Claire Leheny of the National Network of Schools in Partnership (NNSP). Three schools presented on their "2.0" co-endeavors with their local public school systems. Good stuff, with an interesting range of work based on compelling and very thoughtful motivations.

The NNSP is to be commended, at least by me, for its efforts to improve the breed of independent school–public school collaborations. Service learning and "community service," good ideas in their way but historically often short on equality of benefit, have become the lower rungs on a ladder of possibility that now rises pretty far. Focusing especially on the idea of equivalent reciprocal positive purpose, partnership 2.0—as the program put it—is based on deeper levels of institutional commitment: psychically, culturally, and economically. I enjoyed hearing about the work of the Washington (D.C.) International School, Roland Park Country School, and the Latin School of Chicago—worthy, righteous efforts all.

My brain took its own path as Latin School head Randall Dunn described an array of programs designed, at their core, to connect his school with the city around it.

It struck me that Mr. Dunn's school appropriates the name of its city into its own name, and I began to see the school's partnership initiatives as a way to live up to, or maybe even justify, that part of the name—truly to be a school "of Chicago."

This led me to wondering about the scores of independent schools with place-names in their moniker. A couple of years back Cape Cod Academy, for instance, decided to style itself as "Cape Cod's academy," a move that inspired the school actively to seek more (and more welcome) ways to connect with its region so as to be an asset and resource for the Cape.

How many place-named schools could comfortably add apostrophe-s to their names and be honestly representing themselves to be in partnership, symbiosis even, with their eponymous communities? And would this question in fact be a useful guide in helping schools identify urgent and important work that they might be doing in order to authentically be "of" their town, city, or region? Even if their place-name is a geographical feature—a mountain or a bay—might this imply an obligation to engage and steward?

I like this challenge. Of course, in its way it seems to let schools named for people or ideas off the hook, and that's not fair. But surely there might be something in the name of a founder, an idea, or an animal that might be embodied in an aggressive approach to partnership across sectors?

I'd go so far as to suggest that an independent school sharing a place-name with its local public school system might consider that to be a mandate, or at least an invitation, to some serious partnership. Why not dig deep to find those synergies that can enhance the experience of students at both Willowhurst Academy and Willowhurst High School?

And along with partnerships, these partnerships might unlock some extraordinary opportunities for place-based learning. But I guess that's a post for another day.

Not Your Father's School, March 1, 2014

KEEPING KIDS HEALTHY AND SAFE: STRESS, EXPECTATIONS, AND THE LIVES OF STUDENTS

We have been doing a singularly poor job of making kids' lives better of late, as the statistics on adolescent mental health trends show. It's hard to be teenager or pre-teen in our time, pressured by attainment expectations, ever in the harsh spotlight of the performative social media world, and assailed by truly existential threats like social injustice, gun violence, and climate change.

Schools tend to keep kids cooped up for many hours a week as well as involving all manner of performances, academic and otherwise, most of which are subject to some sort of evaluation— win/lose, pass/fail, "like" or not... The stakeholders for most of these are the students themselves and often their families.

Sometimes, though, schools and educators frame themselves as stakeholders. Busy, high-achieving, winning kids reflect well on their schools, and the schools happily bask in the reflected glory of their students who achieve in the most conventionally notable ways. View these students, if you will, as gladiators, winning zero-sum victories in college admission and in other high-visibility, high-prestige arenas. Tell me if you think this is a good thing.

Or we might look at these students, as I suggest below, as child laborers, working long, hard hours on schools' behalf to burnish institutional reputations.

Can we do better? Can we challenge current ideas of "success" and turn the tide on the stress culture we have created and stoked? Others, acknowledging my theft of language from Denise Pope and Making Caring Common, are asking the same questions. Can we, to coopt the words of David Gleason, defend adolescence in the fiercely competitive school cultures we too often exalt?

21

THE FRAGILITY OF CHILDREN AND THE STRENGTH OF COUNSELORS

Kids are fragile; a recent spate of bad news has me ruminating on this fact. Yes, Florida, and yes, the young man from *Glee*, whose rehab experiences started when he was 19. But yes, also, kids on bike trips, kids who have made bad choices in college, and desperate kids who elect to check out before their time.

In independent schools college counselors, as opposed to general guidance or therapeutic counselors, are de rigueur. In my days as a college counselor I regularly encountered a piece of information so startling that it was hard for me to wrap our heads around: the average counseling load in public schools is something over 400 students per counselor. This staggering figure defies any possible rationalization.

It feels as though, like art and music, guidance seems to be regarded—Oh! how wrongly!—as one of those ancillary aspects of education that students and school districts can live without when budgets shrink and student populations soar. Even if the numbers were not so crazy, the average school guidance counselor is responsible for an enormous array of student services: college counseling, general counseling, vocational counseling, drug and alcohol ed, sorting out a world of services for at-risk kids. Any school with a counseling staff that does any one of these things well should be given a standing ovation—and many, many of them do. I can only shake my head in admiration.

The other day I wrote about small schools and <u>very small schools</u>. I also had a funny (odd) conversation with an independent school colleague last week that made me realize both how spoiled I have become and how warped is my sense of scale. As a teacher I have rarely taught a class of more than fifteen students, and I have never worked in a school with more than 80-some students in the largest grade. I've been able to know every kid I've worked with very well, with my own overall student load always something below the old threshold number (80, as it happens) that the Coalition of Essential Schools used to promote as an upper limit for effective education. For me and for many of my colleagues these numbers, 15 and 80, are kind of the defaults of what we assume a teacher should have to handle. I'm pretty sure I could rise to the occasion of larger numbers (I've had elective classes of 20, but that's still pretty small), but I don't suppose I will ever know for sure.

So when I read about guidance counselors having to, and succeeding in, keeping on top of 400 lives (and that's on the low side of average, so there are many counselors with way more than that), I once again find myself wishing that our society had the courage and good sense to commit itself to looking after kids' personal growth in our schools as thoroughly as we seem determined to look after their ability to take standardized tests.

No, more counselors probably wouldn't have saved some of the kids whose stories have been piling up on me in the last few days, but they might have helped many others find direction, strength, and support to make it through the sometimes brutal years of childhood and adolescence.

Because kids are fragile, you know.

"Independent Schools, Common Perspectives," *Education Week*, July 15, 2013

22

DIFFICULT QUESTIONS ABOUT STUDENT STRESS AND ANXIETY

The Independent Curriculum Group make no bones about our concern for the well-being and mental health of students, as nearly every day brings us a worrisome story or anecdote about student stress. Much of this appears to be very much a function of anxiety around the complex constellation of academic and social pressures felt by students working to succeed in the educational system we have created. We wonder about it, and what we as educators might do to make schools happier places for children and adults. Perhaps we're just in alarmist mode, generalizing from specifics, but each time we ask a school person about students in crisis at their school, we get an affirmative response.

So we present to you, readers, some difficult, discomfiting questions. You are invited to take these as either rhetorical or substantive (or both), and to frame your responses—not to us, but to yourselves—but in the context of your learning community accordingly.

Have you or the institution you represent noted and acknowledged an uptick in anxiety and anxiety-related behaviors among students?

Have you or the institution you represent engaged in tactical measures—hiring more counselors, more training of faculty, more...?

Have you or the institution you represent acknowledged likely systemic and situational sources of this uptick in anxiety and anxiety-related behaviors among students?

Have you or the institution you represent considered countermeasures to reduce or ameliorate the systemic conditions that might underlie the uptick in anxiety and anxiety-related behaviors among students?

Following this line of inquiry may invite a kind of "blame game" that can situate responsibility on generalized targets like "the media," "parents," "colleges." If these are apt or common responses (and they may well be), we need to drill down or, paradoxically, to start by ascending to a 30,000-foot level and considering what we do in the broadest sense.

All learning happens in a context, and in the established world of pre-college education we have planted our collective flag atop the mountain of missions and values (think: the accrediting process). We set out with good hearts to create institutions of teaching and learning built around these at least purportedly idiosyncratic, "mission driven" elements:

Cultures of learning comprised schedules, "grading" and assessment systems, administrative hierarchies, reward systems, professional learning expectations, age-cohort- and academic-discipline-related bureaucracies, and co-curricular offerings with their own hierarchies and systems of reward and recognition.

Intentional curricula, ostensibly and hopefully aimed at meeting the requirements of larger systems whose demands are more often perceived through our own institutional and personal lenses than clearly stated "from on high."

Pedagogies that may be innovatively designed or that cautiously default to the hackneyed and clichéd, all providing student learning experiences with as broad a range of efficacies as of types.

Try putting on your skeptic's (or hardcore realist's) glasses and taking a look at the full context of learning at your school. It might be well to reserve some time for deep reflection as you ponder these related and very germane issues:

What is the "null curriculum" in your institution? That is, what is not taught or emphasized, leaving learners to infer that these things are unimportant or even, in some way, taboo or off limits? How might this message, however unintentionally implied, create a kind of cognitive or emotional dissonance in students' minds and hearts?

What about the "hidden curriculum," the ways in which certain structures, policies, sequences, or reward systems send messages about what is important that may be at odds with "official" or proclaimed values and beliefs? Is the very culture or organization of your institution in some way contributing to student apathy, cynicism, or angst?

Consider, for a moment, your school's "best and brightest," the students for whom stellar academic careers and accomplishments are forecast; they who will be, say, future National Merit Scholars or hyperselective college or next-school admits. In the culture of your institution, how are the accomplishments of these students highlighted or rewarded?, In what ways (if any, to be sure) are the expectations placed on these students unlike those placed upon the generality of students.

And in what ways (if any) might resources of certain kinds be directed toward these students in ways not entirely consonant with those "official" or proclaimed values and beliefs? Might this actually create undue or iniquitous pressure or stress that is less about a "student-centered" experience than about the needs or even that exaltation of the institution itself?

Does your school note or acknowledge an "achievement gap" or, equally unsettling, a comfort gap? Are members of certain groups less successful in your school, or do they feel less welcome and included in the culture and the programs? Do individuals in these groups, then—and we would include students, families, and faculty and staff here—experience your school (in any or all of its parts) differently, and perhaps as more stressful, than other members of your community?

There are of course a host of corollary and shadow (as in, "Why not?") questions accompanying each of those asked here, but we'll stop for now.

If you are inclined to explore these questions more deeply, we would point you to these terrific and relevant resources:

Challenge Success, an outgrowth of the work of Denise Pope and others. "We partner with schools, families, and communities to embrace a broad definition of success and to implement research-based strategies that promote student well-being and engagement with learning."

The films of Vicki Abeles, especially *Race to Nowhere* and *Beyond Measure*

At What Cost? Defending Adolescent Development in Fiercely Competitive Schools by David L. Gleason, PsyD

Under Pressure: Confronting the Epidemic of Stress and Anxiety in Girls by Lisa Damour, PhD

The film *Most Likely to Succeed* and the book *What School Could Be: Insights and Inspiration from Teachers Across America* by Ted Dintersmith

Making Caring Common, part of the same Harvard Graduate School of Education project that produced the "Turning the Tide" report. "Collaborating with partners and engaging in national media work to amplify our messages and elevate the importance of developing children's care for others and the common good in our public dialogue."

The Independent Curriculum Blog, January 7, 2019

23

WHATEVER HAPPENED TO "UNANXIOUS" EXPECTATIONS?

Every now and then I like to settle back with a warm, brimming cup of <u>Ted Sizer</u> and ponder how it was when the <u>Coalition of Essential Schools</u> was young and we already worked hard to leave no child behind without Congress having to legislate this, as if it somehow hadn't occurred to us.

Of the principles of the <u>Coalition</u>, the one that always stands out for me, is about decency and trust:

The tone of the school should explicitly and self-consciously stress values of unanxious expectation ("I won't threaten you but I expect much of you"), of trust (until abused) and of decency (the values of fairness, generosity and tolerance).

What a wonderful term, "unanxious expectation;" how much of what troubles us every day and in broader contemplation is embedded in those two words?

Now, I've been an independent school college counselor for a while, and I know all about anxiety and expectations. I'm also the parent of four kids who have gone through what we rather wanly call "the college process;" to many kids, this feels more like an extended session on the rack. I see the effect of this on kids and families, and I do what I can to mitigate the worst of it, focusing on "fit" and "match"—but for the family it still so often comes down to fat or thin envelopes.

A <u>recent article</u> in the *New York Times* reports on research suggesting that stress levels for upper middle class kids are not so different from those affecting poorer children. It's easy to see why: if mommy and daddy are devoting inordinate amounts of time and treasure to giving a kid "every opportunity" to "succeed" in the world of high-stakes education and the admissions beauty pageant that goes with it, how must a child feel when she or he contemplates failure—all that test prep, all those summer programs and community service hours and AP courses, and in the end still a thin envelope?

As a society we are most of us complicit as cheerleaders for a system that is about anything but unanxious expectations. Independent and charter schools proudly roll out and repeat the word "rigorous" in their missions and self-descriptions, with "excellence" (= brag-level accomplishments, no public missteps) close behind. We are fascinated, even when revulsed, by the near-abusive details in the confessions of that Tiger Mom. If we did that to our own kids, we secretly wonder, would they, too, waltz into the Ivy League? Would it be worth it? And admission officers at selective colleges remind kids all the time that admission is a largely function of the "rigor" of their course loads; if your testing isn't so great, just pile on a few more Honors courses.

The syndrome can start with secondary school admissions, or even earlier. Parents in New York City, we are told, bite their nails to the quick while they scheme about pre-school admission and even public kindergarten placement. Poor households fret about making it through the day, and wealthy ones fret about their kids' futures; either way, it's tragically never enough just to be where they are.

And let's talk about homework. Most people still seem to believe that more is better, despite the evidence that great education can occur in its near-total absence. If kids aren't doing lots of math problems or writing papers, people think, they will be rotting their minds on TV or video games. They totally miss that there might be another way of looking at the opportunity costs: instead of craving the anodyne of TV or games to soothe minds and souls frazzled by schoolwork-for-schoolwork's sake, kids with real mental energy left at the end of a school day might actually discover and develop new interests, adding to their cognitive, cultural, creative, and social storehouses in ways even more significant and useful than simply doing six more math problems that are essentially just the first four, warmed over. Allowing kids to explore these interests, Tony Wagner tells us, leads to creating innovators.

Homework-happy teachers may also be part of the problem, but they are also victims.

Whatever bearing my school's college list might have on my future, the stress I feel must pale beside that of teachers awaiting the results of state testing to know their own personal fates. No wonder we hear of classrooms where virtually the only things being taught relate to the testing that will determine the teacher's professional status and even the continued survival of the school.

"I won't threaten you, but I expect much of you." How many of our students and our teachers confidently feel that this expresses the culture of their schools? I only wish that all education, at every level, really were characterized by unanxious expectations—high expectations requiring vigorous and even appropriately rigorous engagement accompanied by respect, compassion, and humanity.

I fear, though, as long as our society continues to make educational attainment feel like a zero-sum game for rich and poor alike, as long as classrooms must be arenas in which students and teachers are pitted against machine-scored tests and inflexible curricula, that the Coalition's lofty principle, like so many other ideals we educators carry around in our hearts, will remain a fantasy.

"Independent Schools, Common Perspectives," *Education Week*, May 15, 2013

24

SCHOOL AND THE INTERESTED CHILD

Another school year begins, and for some children this means a period of dissonance in the transition between the relative freedom of summer break and the regimentation of the school year. Even for home-schooled or un-schooled students, life in the months that comprise for others the academic year is probably more scheduled and more circumscribed than vacation time.

We are a family of schoolteachers, and so for us it is not an article of faith that school is a place of oppression and stultification where rote learning and dreary routine either squelch intellectual curiosity or kill the young soul. As independent school folks we aren't bound by the kinds of state testing regimes that do truly impinge on the freedom of most public school teachers and students, but we do answer to our superiors and our marketplace. Nonetheless, we believe in school.

Some years back I was contacted by the parent of one of our kids' classmates. They were concerned—upset, even—that their child was completing their assigned work with time to spare each evening. What did I think of this, and what did we do about it at our house, where the same situation, they were sure, obtained? (And it did.)

Among independent school parents in Boston(ish), as in most ambitious urban(ish) communities, a nearly unendurable homework load is the sign of a righteous—that is, rigorous—and worthy education, the marker of a "good" school.

I'm afraid I gave the wrong answer, which was that we were delighted that our son had extra time in the evening to be a part of our family and to pursue his own interests. How great that he could be a kid, sitting in the living room and chatting as we watched television, and that he could consume the books he was taking out of the library by the bagful! The conversation soon ended.

We are not fans of extreme homework ordeals, although we were not entirely unhappy when they have occurred for our children from time to time (sometimes as the well-deserved result of some prior inattention to assignment sheets), and we are especially not fans of homework that is repetitive or assigned simply to be homework. We sincerely hope that your child doesn't have much of this, and we urge families to be assertive with teachers when homework loads are oppressive and destructive to family values and student confidence and happiness. Research is beginning to suggest that excessive homework, or even homework at all, is a poor learning tool, but this notion is so counter to prevailing cultural beliefs that it's a tough position to defend. Few schools have the courage to embrace the principle of diminished homework.

We are fans of the idea that children should be allowed the space and resources to be interested even amidst the exigencies of a busy school year. It can be difficult, but we urge families and children alike to make a priority of carving out time, a few minutes a day even, to pursue personal interests, hobbies, and areas of curiosity even against a backdrop of homework and schedule of classes and extracurriculars.

(And let me add, as a former college counselor, that the "extracurriculars" that matter are those about which a student can speak and write with honest passion. The "best" extracurricular is the one that most engages and inspires the student; for the child with real interest, there isn't any hierarchy of activities, most-impressive-to-least. Don't believe your neighbors or the cocktail party "experts" when they try to tell you there is.)

We also offer this tidbit, based on sixty-plus years of observation in our own classrooms: That the most successful students are actually those who are able to look at the material they are studying and find in it—in each topic, and even in each assignment—something that piques their interest, that allows them to bring their own personal curiosity to bear. This can be a stretch ("Do problems 1–17, odd" may not exactly set a child's mind on fire), but somewhere in every topic and every task many students are able to find some tiny (or larger) nugget of interest, something to spur engagement and even original thought, and this engagement and originality are the hallmarks of a successful student.

It may be axiomatic in some quarters that school is a drag, a damper on the spirit, but it doesn't have to be this. Just as we urge the Interested Child to engage with new activities and new ideas, so do we urge them to engage with school—at the same time as they continue to engage with their own continuing exploration of the world and all that it offers.

The Interested Child, September 5, 2014

25

OUR NEW CHILD LABOR SYSTEM AND THE HARM IT'S DOING—LET'S END THIS

How many of our schools lead with their college or next-school lists when they present themselves to the world? How many tout their students' test scores and yield rates as evidence of the quality of the education they provide? And whom, exactly, does this kind of messaging serve?

Once upon a time our forebears heated their homes with coal and wore clothing produced by child labor, and now we help children worry about whether they have enough activities or good enough grades or test scores to get into the college of their dreams—often equally or even more so the college of their families' and their schools' dreams and aspirations. If our students are laboring for sixty or so hours a week to gratify, glorify, and pacify the educational expectations and anxieties of others, how different is this from 60 hours a week "in the hole" or in the mills on behalf of the robber barons of yore?

But this is the least of our worries. The mental health crisis that we are experiencing in high-pressure, competitive schools, independent or public, is driving more and more students to fear school and to take anti-social and even self-destructive measures to relieve their agonies. Ten years ago we heard relatively few reports of students taking time out of school for mental health-related reasons. Now I hear of few schools where this is not a frequent occurrence. Across the country we hear of student suicides related at least in part to academic stress and anxiety.

I've used this space to share my own anxieties about the future of the world and the future of education. I may sound a bit shrill, but I'm scared for all kids. It's bad enough that existential threats to democracy, to humanity, and to life on the planet itself seem to be multiplying, providing a backdrop that now rivals or surpasses the fears of my adolescent self in the most nuclear-fraught years (atmospheric tests, Cuba; duck-and-cover) of the Cold War. But add to this a toxic cultural cocktail of apathy, hysteria, overt bigotry, selfish greed, mistrust, and astounding economic disparities, and you have a tough world in which to be any age, much less young.

And a tough world in which to be an educator. If it's not about distractions, it's about deprivations or fears, and amidst it all we're asked to be experts in curriculum design, in assessment, and in the neurodevelopmental characteristics of children. We must teach with justice and global awareness as we leverage an ever-evolving array of tech tools and new practices. We understand the imperatives, and we work our tails off to rise to every occasion, and yet at the same time we are sometimes forced to wonder if we are complicit in maintaining a harmful system.

It's not just about class and race and privilege, though these things play an enormous role in the crisis. If college admission pressure, for example, might look like a "First World problem," at least in the media and on the cocktail party circuit, we cannot ignore the differential experiences of all groups, privileged and not, in their deep concerns around educational access and quality. We can try to create mini-utopias on our campuses, where lofty values and multicultural harmony prevail (at least on the surface) or at least outweigh a baser ethos within whatever spatial, temporal, and even digital boundaries we may establish. But when our students experience and act in the world, there is no zone of proximate morality to buffer them from injustice, inequity, and hatred—or violence.

I have mused on the idea of a Grand Unified Theory of education that would bring together the essences—and urgencies—of current thinking and practice around social justice, mindfulness, anti-racism, student mental health, independent curriculum, and educational access and equity. There are plenty of people and organizations working on these things piecemeal and plenty of schools that are up to their eyeballs in multiple facets of this great, convoluted conceptual mass. But we need to figure out a way to bring together the best minds and most passionate spirits in the service of concerted, connected action. Progress in this area is not just important, it's a moral imperative.

Who ought to be in the room for this? I've got my list, but who's on yours? How do we make this happen?

The Independent Curriculum Blog, November 27, 2017

CLASSROOMS OF TRUTH AND EQUITY: CHALLENGES OF OUR TIMES

We want to believe that our classrooms and campuses and even their digital extensions are places where truth and fairness reign, although we are keenly aware of the role that falsehood, coercion, and injustice play in the daily lives of students, socially and culturally. We have handbooks and rules and principles and values on which we can call in the name of righteousness, and we even have laws in many jurisdictions that are written to protect students from "bullying" in its many forms. We know that we live in a hurting and sometimes hating world.

We exhort one another and our students to stand up against the evils of the world, to speak out in the spirit of Martin Niemöller's exhortation to look beyond ourselves and our own interests in the quest for justice. But even when cases seem extreme, it's not easy, as the weight of our institutions and special interests within them can chill the most righteous of impulses, and we can be paralyzed by the world's increasingly baffling ethical complexity. Coupled with educators' and students' highly attuned hypocrisy radar, it's not often easy to know when and how to exercise personal morality in a world that seems to let quite a lot of ickiness slide right by.

But strong we must be, and we cannot back down from either the truth or the power to which it must be spoken.

26

CONFRONTING STUDENT PREJUDICE: IMPORTANT QUESTIONS ABOUT A SCHOOL'S OBLIGATION TO ADDRESS HATEFUL OR HURTFUL EXPRESSION; DO YOUR VALUES HAVE TEETH?

A history teacher encounters a dismissive and demeaning reference to gay and lesbian people in a student essay. A Spanish teacher senses that students are obliquely mocking stereotypes of Latinx persons during conversational practice exercises. An English student continually asserts in class discussions of a Toni Morrison novel that white people are an imperiled minority.

These are teachable moments, right?

The teacher must call on the students to justify their statements with facts or counterarguments, reminding them in teacherly ways that such expressions might be painful to some listeners or readers. Operating within the constraints of the "free speech rights" of the student versus the teacher's obligation to protect fact and uphold the values of the school, the dialogue or debate must go forward, counter-argument against counter-argument, until some kind of stasis—maybe just an agreement to disagree—is reached.

But when, confronted with obvious evidence, can a teacher call out behavior or expression as racist or as expressing a kind of bias that is at odds not only with the teacher's own values but those implicit or explicit in the school's statements of values and beliefs? Is this ever the right thing to do, and can a teacher reasonably expect that a school administration will back them up?

And it's not just students, we know. A faculty member might hold and express biased perspectives on certain groups of people, subtly and infrequently expressed well beyond the sight or earshot of students, but nonetheless painful to colleagues.

It's easy for schools to address anonymous or flagrant bias incidents: the note on the locker, the social media post, the abhorrent photograph. The leadership appropriately musters the community's righteous indignation, reminds everyone that there is no place for this kind of thing, and perhaps even separates members caught red-handed in behavior that is patently and intentionally hurtful to others. All this is as easy as expelling the students caught vaping in a bathroom where *This Is A Non-Smoking Campus*.

But let's say that a student or students are well known in the community for living in a household where prejudiced perspectives are the norm. Either because the school didn't know about or ignored these oppositional values during the admission process or because the household in question has some authority in or special value to the school as an institution, the children of the household arrive at school each day armed with beliefs that might be inflammatory but shielded by their special privilege from the consequences of expressing these beliefs. To confront these students of "parents of power," as I call them, is to risk one's job, and every private school teacher knows it.

We exhort independent schools, in particular, to live by their missions and values, to build their communities and cultures of learning around high ideals embodied in lofty mission statements and positive assertions. In our most optimistic moments we can imagine that these statements and the supporting evidence schools provide in their marketing and advancement messaging comprise a covenant between schools and families: a solemn, high-stakes promise made and to be kept by the school.

But in whose name do we create these aspirational statements? Is it for the institution as a corporate entity, a "we" that offers a side-door through which contrary-minded individuals, in the moment or in their own committed beliefs, can usher themselves without consequence? Or are these aspirational statements of values and purposes (or should they be) intended as benign but rock-hard imperatives that serve as the moral and ethical foundation of intentional communities?

Does your school's enrollment contract explicitly connect supporting your school's mission and values to community membership? Does your board's "Statement on Diversity" (perhaps now looking a bit long in the tooth, as many of these are) commit not just the institution but its members—faculty, students, and families alike—to abiding by its expressed principles of equity and inclusion?

In other words, do or should school's statements of values and purposes have any teeth? Can a student be confronted not just with the illogic of a biased position but with the ways in which such positions clash with and undermine the ideals of the community? Can students and families legitimately be asked to check protective privilege at the schoolhouse door as antithetical to stated ideals around diversity, equity, and inclusion?

Might offended and uncomfortable teachers reasonably expect that, beyond having to make their personal case to individual students against hurtful or hateful expressions, their schools will support them by addressing these expressions not just as classroom issues but as institutional ones?

No school, of course, can address such questions to any positive effect in the absence of its own community understandings of norms and values around DEI issues. No student can be meaningfully confronted about hurtful expression if the school has not engaged in community-wide conversations and professional learning that provide tools and language for discussing these issues. If the school has an office charged with oversight of such conversations and learning, so much the better, but the work must be everyone's. No effective remonstrance can be issued in the absence of a palpable sense that certain affirmative values are the way "we"—the institution and its individual members—are and must expect themselves to be.

Schools must truly live by the courage of their convictions. If such things matter to a school as much as most schools say they do, the school must be committed to calling out—and perhaps calling the question on—expression that violates its stated ideals. When teachable moments in a classroom don't or can't teach, the institution and all that it stands for must be prepared and willing to step up and step in.

Not Your Father's School, March 16, 2019

27

THE FERGUSON SYLLABUS: TALKING ABOUT SOCIAL JUSTICE WITH KIDS

Readers of *The Interested Child* blog, whose audience is primarily parents and guardians, may or not take an active interest in issues of social justice, which tend to reside (as we confess that we do) on the progressive end of the political spectrum. But it would be hard for anyone in the parenting or educational business to have missed the tsunami of responses to the events in Ferguson, Missouri, in the wake of the shooting by police of Michael Brown.

The shooting and subsequent community unrest have highlighted any number of issues, from the nature of policing to the extent to which racism is bred in the bone of American society. For high-minded rationalists, the civil unrest is a symptom of something complex and nuanced, and for those who lead from the heart in response to the death of a young, unarmed African American man, these events are indicative of a deep and festering wound in the soul of American society.

For the parents and teachers of interested children, the Ferguson situation seems to require some kind of response; children who pay attention to current events will have questions from which it is hard to turn away. This matter has very much been on the minds of educators, who have tried hard—ourselves among them—to consider the most honest and direct ways of responding to these questions while balancing a teacher's responsibility to promote thoughtful inquiry against the equally compelling civic obligation to call out injustice and advocate for justice.

To this end—and I know that some of our readers here are in the home-school world and may not be attuned to discourse in the traditional school community—we would like to call attention here to an accumulating resource for talking to and teaching kids of various ages, developmental stages, and perspectives about the events that we now refer to simply as "Ferguson."

If you are familiar with Twitter—and it's actually a pretty worthy resource for information and ideas relating to educational interests—you may know and understand the "hashtag" concept: that certain topics can be tracked or searched for by hashtag, which is simply a topic name, compressed to a single character string, preceded by the pound sign (#). Thus, anyone with a Twitter account can search or follow the tag (for example) #RedSoxNation (caps optional) to keep tabs on what Boston Red Sox fans are thinking about. Trending events, whether in the news, sports, or entertainment areas, quickly generate their own hashtags, and #Ferguson has been viral in recent days.

Educators, eager to gather resources or teaching about "Ferguson," have created the hashtag #FergusonSyllabus as an identifier for ideas, materials, readings, and approaches to bringing Ferguson-related issues and events into their classrooms. For parents of interested children, as well, a search on #FergusonSyllabus on Twitter will yield useful resources. And if you are home-schooling your child, then the resource will be doubly valuable.

We try to stay away from politics here, but the fact is that the events in Ferguson have struck a chord in educational circles that seem to require a response, and so we offer the #FergusonSyllabus as one way for those who are raising and who work with interested children to explore the many serious questions the events in Missouri have been raising for so many of us.

Incidentally, if this inspires you to take the plunge into Twitter, you can follow us there @interestedchild.

The Interested Child, August 23, 2014

28

HISTORICAL PERSPECTIVE AND A CALL TO ACTION

I wrote this post—slightly edited here—on my personal blog almost five years ago, responding then to the plight of immigrant children and hoping to spur some action on their behalf. THINGS ARE FAR, FAR MORE DREADFUL—AND DEADLY—TODAY, with the United States under its current regime maintaining the equivalent of concentration camps for children in which they are deprived of such basic human and developmental necessities such as soap and a balanced diet. This not only violates all the principles of human decency but also qualifies as child abuse. I call here on all teachers to step up and use their technical status as mandated reporters of abuse, neglect, and cruelty, to raise the hue and cry across the land to report our government's abuse of these children to the proper and duly constituted authorities.

We cannot allow our leaders' contempt for these children and their families to justify depriving of them of their most fundamental human rights and needs—in our name.

I present here a bit of history; as a nation we have long used race, citizen status, and other spurious and specious factors to justify the systemic abuse of children.

This has to stop. Teachers, PLEASE use your voices to report this abuse!

The teaching profession and most of the non-profit and social service sector operate on an assumption that has seemed unassailable to me all of my life: that human beings innately and inherently love and value children above the lives of adults, above all things. "Women and children first!" into the lifeboats; evacuate the kids when the bombs begin to fall.

The other day it struck me, cruelly and horribly, that this is a false premise on which to base either social policy or even, heaven help me, my own life and work.

It boils down to a review of the facts, whether they are to be found watching the news or reading history books. Time after time, in episode after episode, we see overwhelming evidence of a callousness that devalues and dehumanizes children, in particular children of "the Other," and even sacrifices these children wholesale. And human beings, pretty much all kinds of them, have a remarkable facility for designating those not of their tribe or nation or race or faith or class as "the Other."

Human rights campaigns notwithstanding, governments, societies, ostensibly benevolent institutions like churches, and of course individuals have shown themselves capable of both shocking active cruelty and appalling neglect toward children. This isn't news to anyone, but what is compelling and dispiriting to ponder is that such behavior is neither anomalous nor something that humanity is evolving away from.

I think the roots lie in racism, but they lie also in classism and perhaps even in our psychology. For example, the children abused, sometimes to death, in orphanages and in the dark corners of churches have not always been obviously "the Other," but as I understand it, in most cases their vulnerability has stemmed from economic or family dysfunction that left them at the mercy of those designated as their caregivers. The bodies exhumed at the Dozier School in Florida in summer of 2014 are of children to whom society paid no attention or felt so little obligation that their deaths didn't even register to anyone outside the closed, cruel circle of the place. This story is not unusual; it's just the one on the front pages most recently. A century ago, if there'd been a newspaper with the nerve or heart to write them, they might have been similar tales of the Native American boarding schools in the United States and Canada.

In 1940 the school where I work took in, as did a number of American schools, children who had been shipped "across the pond" by their British families to evade Nazi bombs. The Nazis weren't especially singling out children—despite the hundreds of thousands of them who died in the Holocaust—but they weren't interested in protecting them, either. The trans-Atlantic child evacuations ended when a German U-Boat sank the *City of Benares*, a passenger ship carrying 90 children to "safety" in North America. All but thirteen died. The Hitler regime accused the British of using the children as something like a "human shield," and they torpedoed the ship anyway.

I have been haunted since college by a line I encountered in a course on the trans-Mississippi West, perhaps the most horrible—and revealing—words in American history: "Nits make lice." With these three words, U. S. cavalry commander John Milton Chivington justified his orders to murder and mutilate Cheyenne and Arapaho children in what is called the Sand Creek Massacre in 1864. Most history books don't even have the guts to call it, as some do, the Chivington Massacre.

Chivington's sentiment, that the children of enemies, of the Other, grow up to be bothersome adults, seems to offer an explanation for the attitudes that keep bullets flying, rockets falling, and drones buzzing across our 21st-century world. They certainly illuminate the genocidal mindset as I understand it, back as far into history as we are capable of peering. Forget about economics or ideology or even faith. The child of my enemy, of him or her whom I despise, is my enemy, is despicable, is unworthy of life. When humans decide to kill, we start there.

That's about as grim and terrible as the story gets, maybe, but in our own country in our own time we are witnessing the re-segregation of our schools by race and income level and the inevitable disparities in access to resources and opportunity that follow from this. Millions of American children live in poverty, lack adequate food and health care, and attend under-resourced and even physically dangerous schools. We can sing all we want that "children are our future," but kids living in such circumstances are being systemically and systematically denied the chance to participate as equals in that future with their more affluent coevals.

All the worse, of course, for children who lack the legal protections of citizenship: demagogues and a whole lot of average citizens, just plain folks, seem fine with shipping the 50,000 or so recently arrived undocumented children back to whatever murderous, impoverished places they have come from. Would it be different if they were orphans from a plague in Monte Carlo or Copenhagen, carrying their bankbooks in their pale hands?

I'm all for keeping up the positive sentiments around children and the future, but I think we need to take a cold hard look at the world and see that, against all our benevolent and hopeful reckoning, we as a species are perfectly comfortable depriving children of life, liberty, and happiness—not to mention family and opportunity and dignity—with scarcely the batting of an eye.

This means (as so many Dickens novels teach us in the long, gripping, painful parts that precede the happy endings), that those of us who would be reformers, who would put ourselves out there to protect and save and teach the children, are up against a world that cares much less for its children and their lives than we want to believe. We're going to have to revisit our happy-talk notions of human nature and understand that there really are a lot of people who don't actually care whether the children of the poor or of some putative enemy grow up poor, too—or whether they grow up at all.

The Independent Curriculum Blog, June 22, 2019

29

MY CHALLENGE TO SCHOOLS

Stories of schools transformed and students' lives transformed are always inspiring and always thought-provoking. Fare on transformational teachers has infused my life from *The Blackboard Jungle* to *Conrack* to *Les Choristes*, but transformational schools are another matter. From Ted Sizer's *Horace* books to watching a video about Central Park East Secondary School that pointed me toward Deborah Meier's *The Power of Their Ideas*, I have read, as a part of my own transformation as an educator, a succession of books that have made me ever more committed to some of the ideas and ideals they espouse. Just this summer I have read Dennis Littky's *The Big Picture* and *Transforming Schools* by Bob Lenz, Justin Wells, and Sally Kingston.

Because I can be a little slow to see the obvious, it has taken me until about now to realize something that should have been as plain as the nose on my face: All these tales of transformation are about schools whose student communities are on the south side of the American socioeconomic curve. These stories matter so vitally to us because they offer the promise of reducing achievement gaps and redeeming lives failed in multiple ways by systems that have turned their back on America's poor and underserved, their families and their children.

The inspiring narrative has common characteristics, starting with dismal conditions: kids at risk and often woefully below grade-level in essential skills and knowledge, families disengaged and even frightened, expectations as low as the acme of the American Dream is stratospheric. Solutions: new management, or perhaps a new school, with new ideas and new beliefs; new practices and a new culture of learning.

Happy outcomes: graduation rates rise, proud first-in-family stories.

And this is great. It's outstanding, and it's wonderful for those kids and families, and it truly is inspirational.

Now, I don't believe that my readers here represent a big swath of the demographic that these stories are about. Whether you're a casual reader, a friend, or someone from an Independent Curriculum Group Partner trying to figure out what I'm all about, chances are pretty good you're at an independent school that serves a population more likely to reflect *The Emperor's Club* than *To Sir, With Love*. But these stories inspire us still—maybe they play on a certain guilt even as they give us good ideas.

And they are very good ideas. Take *Transforming Schools*, for example, which details the process by which Envision Schools make project-based learning the basis of a rigorous, engaging curriculum and teaching culture that seems to being out the best in kids even as it prepares them for college—and the California higher education system in particular—at rates that confound all previous expectations.

Independent schools, for the most part tend to prepare kids for college at rates that absolutely conform to expectations. Whether a school is straight out of Dickens or innovative as the dickens, independent schools exist to prepare generally affluent and ambitious students from affluent and ambitious families for selective college admission, with the presumption that once matriculated they will have the skills—if not always the will—to succeed. The happy ending is foreordained; the eye-catching stories the media and entertainment industries tell about our schools are almost always about our supposedly anomalous failures.

But what if—and many readers may be about to jump up and say, *But we are! We are!*—an independent school, a St. Basalt's or Jolly Valley Country Day, were to wholly, fully embrace the ideas and practices, from start to finish, of one of these transformational, inspirational schools?

What if we were to admit the possibility that our own students, however accomplished and able they might be, however many generations of college attainment underlie their current success, might still have room for even greater, grander transformations? What if we gave our own students the opportunity to live, say, the culture and program that changes lives at the Envision Schools? What if our teachers, rather than happily assuming that all will be well, push all their students as hard as the Envision Schools push theirs—through real failure and authentic success?

I'd sure like to see that happen. I'd go so far as to challenge the independent school community and beyond to embrace and live the philosophies and practices that seem to have worked so well in schools with less privileged student bodies. What more could our best students do? How might the students on the wrong side of our own achievement gaps be inspired really to take the leaps we dream of for them?

So, is your school ready to take the challenge? To have the faculty and board read *Transforming Teaching* (for example) and then do it, soup to nuts?

Because here's another thing that has occurred to me, late as usual, but powerfully: The argument for these transformational practices is compelling and backed by experience, but in a small sample. But if these ideas were put into practice in other kinds of schools, if evidence could be produced that these practices will work not just for "at risk" kids but for *every* kid, then we would have a case for giving up this testing and accountability 2.0 madness. Along with CPESS, the Met, the Envision Schools, and all their cousins, St. Basalt's and Jolly Valley Country Day could be a part of legitimizing manifestly effective practice and showing the nation and the world that engaging, complex, problem- and project-based learning is not just what "poor kids" need but what every kid needs.

How about it? Are you ready to even consider this?

Not Your Father's School, August 26, 2015

30

CELEBRATING THE HUMAN FACTOR IN OUR WORK

It's the time of year when back-to-school displays show up when you're in the drugstore looking for calamine lotion or sunblock; too early, but the clock is ticking.

It's also the time when new-teacher orientation programs start to happen—just the other day I was privileged to Skype into a fine one taking place at the Bryn Mawr School in Baltimore. And in my own world, it's time for the annual update to my school's *Teacher's Guide to Life and Work*. Each year it gets a little bigger, each year we try to nail down a bit more necessary guidance for our whole faculty, new and veteran.

Thinking about the Bryn Mawr group, or about the ninety or so folks for whom our *Teacher's Guide* is written, I can't help recalling a number of conversations I've had over the years with people who are all excited about some new canned curriculum or other. To these people, and to I suspect a whole lot of others in the educational policy and educational publishing worlds, the ideal would be to create the perfect "teacher-proof curriculum."

In the teacher-proof curriculum, I suppose, all human variables would be removed. No fault in teacher knowledge, no erroneous emphasis would imperil student mastery. The material would be delivered and assessed so tidily that no student could fail to learn. And even the most ho-hum teacher could be assured of pedagogical success.

Thinking of the time we spend training and mentoring teachers and pondering all the verbiage with which we attempt to expound and explain our policies, practices, and even our school culture in the *Teacher's Guide*, I believe it's safe to say that not only is teacher-proof curriculum a silly notion, but that as an ideal it's a bunch of hooey.

We know intuitively that great learning is often based on great relationships, and that in the K–12 world the teachers who can get the most out of students are the teachers who get their students the most. This means that the whole idea of de-personalizing the teaching enterprise is an easy path not to success but to educational failure. A curriculum delivered devoid of the humanity of an engaged teacher is no curriculum at all; it's a *Wikipedia* page or, worse still, a script.

It's axiomatic that no amount of teacher orientation and no amount of carefully written explanation can prepare a teacher for all of the challenges and opportunities that present themselves, scattershot, at the start of a school year. The best-prepared new teachers still occasionally find themselves feeling like deer in the headlights, not because they're not clever or weren't paying attention to their mentors, but because school is hard, up-close-and-personal work, with every decision freighted with somebody's emotional "stuff." Even the most straightforward material has subtleties requiring sensitive and responsive teaching. You can't teacher-proof curriculum, because you can't (and wouldn't want) to teacher-proof school.

Even the politicos and self-styled experts whose ideas of "school reform" include expressed contempt for teachers know this is true, and they tacitly admit it every time they call for schools of education to accept only academically top-flight candidates. They know as well as we do that teachers matter, and that teacher-proof curriculum is no curriculum at all.

What we need, in every sector, is curriculum that is infused with the blood, sweat, and passion of teachers, passion that turns mere "intended learning outcomes" into transformational experiences. We don't need automata in our classrooms, meting out learning in doses prescribed and prepackaged by giant publishers and testing companies. We need teachers who are confident being fully and energetically themselves, expert in designing for their students demanding, exciting curriculum that inspires and challenges and equally expert in developing assessments that measure in-depth understanding, not just rote knowledge or received "truths."

No matter how much detail I use to explain certain aspects of school policy in our *Guide*, and no matter how carefully we "orient" new teachers to our schools, we can never fully capture nor really begin to transmit the full complexity of just about every aspect of what we do. We can't "proof" our teachers against all the fluid and ambiguous realities of working with kids. Even if we could, we would lose something vital from the cultures of our schools. We can make our *Teacher's Guide* as detailed as we like, but we know that at best it is only a guide; it can never be a blueprint or a script.

All we can do, and all we can expect to do, is to prepare our new teachers for the big, obvious things, and then be there for them when little things and delicately shaded nuances show up and startle them. Another truism about school life, in my experience, is that very few things happen in exactly the same way twice; kids and circumstances always seem to tend toward the novel and surprising.

Instead of trying to teacher-proof our curricula and remove the human element from what we do, we need to be better at recognizing and cultivating the human connections and the human factor in our work. It is after all because we are human that we have schools at all; the human heart, mind, body, and soul comprise an engine of enormous power that we need to fully harness, not minimize, in the educational endeavor.

"Independent Schools, Common Perspectives," *Education Week*, July 24, 2013

31

"WE TEACH": THE ELUSIVE LANGUAGE OF CHARACTER EDUCATION

While I was in the middle of thinking about <u>my own Six C's for Learning</u>, a hot conversation was taking place in one of the online college counseling communities about the ways in which schools report—or choose not to report—disciplinary infractions to colleges.

At least one school stated that reporting such incidents to colleges, and making sure that students are aware that such reports will be made, is an aspect of "character education" at the school.

Huh.

I get it, and I know perfectly well what they mean and how this fits in with the ways in which many if not most educators understand character education at its lowest common denominator—the utility of a strongly stated rule and its consequences: a bit of a threat, say, something to disincentivize (there's a word Orwell would have loved!) wrongful behavior. Students learn the rules and the penalties, and they make better decisions. Arguably, this is the way the world works, and always has.

Many schools claim, explicitly or as nearly so as can be, that they educate character. I think that all schools do, somehow, educate character, but when I write about it I am often struck by the limitations of language in helping us explain or describe, exactly, how this happens.

For example, do we "instill" or "teach" or "foster" values? Or do we create environments in which values grow by themselves, perhaps in channels we have somehow prepared—intentionally or not—that lead in directions we,

111

or our institutions, favor? Do we use the active voice, as in "we create an environment in which students develop" or "we teach," or do we choose more passive constructions: "values are instilled" or "students are taught" or "students at our school learn"? Do we adopt the hortatory when laying out desirable actions and values: "You should" or "Thou shalt not" or even the mushier "You probably don't want to" or "You might like to"?

And there is the question of modeling. Do we, really? Anecdotal evidence says yes, but how much of our "modeling" is intentional or explicit, and how much subtle, unintentional—and perhaps even antithetical to our aims and own core values? If students do as I do and not as I say, will I approve of the result? What lessons are learned from the coach whose R-rated mutterings at a referee are audible to a few of the kids on the bench, even if the coach does not want to confront the official? What do my students learn when I can't keep my promises about returning graded work?

Vance Wilson and Steve Clem reminded independent schools in their classic _Paths to New Curriculum_ (1991) about the "null curriculum"—things that are "taught" because their opposites or converses are not: Think of a school in which the heckling of an opposing team's athletes is not explicitly discouraged at the instance, and the "lesson" students (at both schools) might "learn" from this. Most of the null curriculum is about values—character education often occurs in negative space, if you will.

Honor Codes, for the most part, make me think long and hard. What is "Honor" with a capital H, exactly? How do we define it? In many schools it seems to be primarily rolled into discussions of academic honesty, which is one kind of honor but seems (to me) a rather reductive, even negative, conception of the idea; honor codes used in these ways become more about what not to do—at worst, they're just self-inflicted regimes of enforcement: "You signed this!"—than definitions of idealized behavior. I try not to think about so-called "honor killings" in this context. I know that at a few schools the Honor Code really is about ideals and that it truly enhances community; I wish this were always the case, at least from what I hear.

Mostly, I'm just leery of any absolute claim made by any school that it instills or teaches or in some way actively, explicitly, and successfully inculcates "values" or "character" in some concrete, definable way. In all schools, I know and deeply believe, students do develop character and values along lines that are consonant or congruent with certain values that the school promulgates; this is the center of our value proposition, in my opinion, and it tends to work out pretty well. About the best I can do for a statement of cause-and-effect, however, is something along the lines of "Our school provides an environment and intentionally designed experiences in which we hope and intend for students to grow and internalize our core institutional values of integrity, compassion, intellectual engagement, and humility (or what have you)."

But how we talk about the process by which this happens, and how we connect the dots between what we intend and do and what results, is a good deal more subtle, idiosyncratic, and hard to define than assertions about the connection between discipline reporting and character education.

My personal experience in conversations with adults suggests that the best character education happens in schools where there is some comfort—uncomfortable as this always is in the moment—with gray areas and moral messiness. School cultures purportedly built around absolutes seem to create sharp edges that can cut in many more ways and from more directions than people anticipate—and leave lasting scars. Humility and flexibility seem to go a lot farther than do "zero tolerance policies" in teaching—or creating environments and experiences that promote or nourish—positive values.

And before you remind me that some things must be absolutes, I'm talking here about values—about what the student understands to be right and wrong—and not about specific behaviors. Sometimes behaviors cross a line, but in the end serious misbehavior is seldom—never, probably—about values alone.

Independent schools need to understand clearly that their significant difference from other kinds of institutions is their explicit aim to connect with each student in a personal way—in small classes, on teams, in advisor groups, in clubs, in dormitories. Just as each school purports to stand for something through its mission, core values, and in some cases through connection with a spiritual or philosophical tradition, schools want—and parents want—to have each graduate stand for something, too. Each element of a school's culture and programming must support this in a well understood way, and deep personal relationships seem to be a primary source of this support.

Of course, each student is unique, bringing to school each day a set of personal, home-based values as well as a psyche shaped by experience in ways that no one can fully understand—not to mention the dreams and aspirations they bring. Great schools, I believe, create environments in which the best aspects of each child are explored, revealed, nurtured, reinforced, and sometimes challenged. To do this, schools themselves have to know and be confident in who they are and what they aspire to be for their students in order that the culture and the values embedded in it will be transmitted—passive voice here, I note—naturally to all members of the community, all the time.

Not Your Father's School, December 13, 2012

32

THE SENSITIVITY GAP

As an educator, a some-time college counselor, and the parent of college-age kids, I watch with great interest the various morality plays unfolding on college campuses—many of these on so-called "elite" college campuses. Between trigger warnings, micro-aggressions, and the spread of awareness of sexual assault and harassment, students on college campuses these days are receiving a profound education in how words and actions can hurt others, an education nuanced far beyond the "sticks and stones," "can't say you can't play," and "no means no" lessons learned on playgrounds and in middle-school sex ed classes.

I read about and appreciate these stories in the educational trade journals and occasionally the mainstream media. But it has occurred to me that young Americans who do not attend college, at least full time, or who do not live on college campuses are not being taught these lessons, nor are they living in communities in which their import and impact is felt on a minute-to-minute basis. The majority of young Americans, like the vast majority of their elders, do not live in a world where speech is circumscribed by worries related to micro-aggression or cultural appropriation or where each interaction is conditioned by a learned and heightened desire to not offend or frighten.

It is perhaps no wonder that the Trumps and trumpkins of our world are baffled and apparently offended by the niceties of what they sneeringly call "political correctness." They see a special code of detailed and ever-evolving rules and principles that look to those not steeped in them like a kind of moral minuet—effete, elitist, a left-wing puritanism that looks down upon their every impulse to say or even think what they may say and think. That "p.c" might just stand first and foremost for heightened politeness and courtesy seems a foreign concept.

Yesterday I listened to moderately conservative *Boston Globe* columnist Alex Beam practically asphyxiate on his own words after he expressed in passing his preference for English as an "official" U. S. language on a public radio talk show. The liberal host judiciously left Beam to twist in the chilly wind of his own awareness of the disapproval this idea would meet from a public radio audience. Everyone got that the joke, or the onus, in this context was on Beam. But it was most assuredly a conclave—radio participants and listeners—of the educated and informed, responding to a sort of "First World" moral dilemma.

What do American college students deeply enmeshed in their controversies and conversations on sex, race, speech, and justice think when they consider the rest of their nation? Does their heightened moral awareness separate them even more from the generality of their fellow citizens? As an educated minority that is almost by definition an economically privileged minority, does their differential experience and awareness of racism and sexism and the meaning of these create yet another chasm of separation between them and the mass of the nation's people?

Normally here I would call upon our K–12 schools to step up their educational efforts in these "nuanced" areas of political and cultural sensitivity, but it's not entirely schools' job; and anyhow the audience here tends to be independent schools, already a self-separating "elite" (if you want to use that term) in itself. I think that the work must mostly be done by the media, both topical and pure entertainment versions, who could start by not treating issues like the renaming of college buildings, inadequate sentences for sexual assault, or the fall-out from the University of Chicago's stance on trigger warnings *et al.* like the birth of a three-headed calf: exotic, rare, and with just enough of an ick factor to the general public to sell newspapers. The media could simply start asking and even reminding us when some things are really not okay to say and do.

In the meantime maybe colleges could add to their (often commendably self-imposed) tribulations in all this some education of their students on how to think about and respond to injustices and aggressions, micro and otherwise, in the world beyond their campuses. We cannot afford as a society to have any more ways in which a few people (who often look a lot like me and mine, I admit), the putatively "enlightened," can permit themselves to look down upon and judge those who have less—be it money, power, privilege, education, or sensitivity.

Not Your Father's School, September 9, 2016

VOICES IN THE WILDERNESS?
ADVOCATING FOR A BETTER WORLD

Disingenuousness about beliefs and their expression has been part of independent school culture from the beginning. Advocacy of causes and expression of ideas outside a very narrow mainstream was so unlikely and so frowned upon that for all intents and purposes such causes and ideas might not have existed at all. Muscular Christianity and conventional patriotism—keeping to the right of class traitor Franklin Roosevelt!—*would provide students with all the values they would ever need. Anti-Semitic and racist admission policies relieved schools of the burden of inclusion and even the consideration of civil rights and multiculturalism.*

In my working lifetime many educators have tried to turn the corner on such attitudes, and we've tried to bring schools around with us. In these essays I try to speak up and speak out on behalf of speaking up and speaking out. Injustice, cruelty, and apathy must be called out, and what better place to begin than by encouraging the voices of rising generations to join and then to lead the myriad choirs of freedom?

But what about free speech? *some will ask.* What about my right not to hear things with which I disagree or that make me uncomfortable?

Just. Born. Too. Late.

Sorry.

33

EQUITY IN EDUCATION: LET'S ELEVATE OUR EXPECTATIONS!

(This essay has been partly inspired by my recent reading of Anand Giridharadas's Winners Take All *and Steven Brill's* Tailspin. *Both books should be on every educator's #MustRead list. The essay appeared originally in the Independent Curriculum Group's March 2018 newsletter.)*

I have been encountering too many things in books and in the news that worry me about the fate of our planet. Rising inequalities, in particular, have become a constant gut-punch. To begin with, I must own my privilege, the goodie bag of cultural capital I tote around as a white, aging, cis male and as a beneficiary of a "meritocracy" built on educational attainment in a system one of whose chief gatekeepers has been standardized testing.

The winners in this "meritocracy" have been nurturing and rewarding their own now for several generations, and the numbers tell us that my cohort and our children—if not each of us personally—are holding an increasingly disproportionate share of the world's wealth. Authors like Anand Giridharadas and Steven Brill and political figures like Alexandria Ocasio-Cortez and Bernie Sanders keep asking insistent questions about this, and I have been wondering how our system of education might hold itself accountable for its role in creating and sustaining inequity. Even more, musing on the ideals and aspirations embodied in so many of our schools' mission statements and the caring values of the educators I know, I have been trying to figure out how the education sector might become a powerful voice in the work of making things better.

I have spent my life in and around independent schools, places of privilege and affluence, and I have a sense of those

119

who believe in and attend such places. Those with access to these schools share some fundamental beliefs about the nature of school and education:

They believe in school as a place where all things that happen will be instrumental goods in the lives of students.

They believe that the tall and benevolent ladder of education carries upward lives whose material and social prospects are measured by the number of rungs climbed and the quality of the ascent—and who see few if any limits on this number or this quality.

They look to schools to provide ever-improving ways for learning to occur and ever more creative and instrumentally useful kinds of learning experiences.

They expect schools to be places of safety where each student is known and cared about.

They expect schools to be places that draw out and refine the best characteristics of children and young adults.

They expect schools to create conditions whereby engagement and enjoyment will be a natural part of their cultures and curricula.

They expect that this engagement and enjoyment, provided in the context of an appropriately high degree of challenge, will lead to the reward of adult lives of meaning and satisfaction.

They believe and expect that all of these things will come to pass.

These attitudes certainly should not shock us. But above all they should not be held solely by those who can afford private schools or who live in communities with public schools tied in to the same meritocracy. Why should not every family in every community have the right to believe and expect the same for every child?

Why is it not our greatest, most urgent national project to create a society whose highest goal is for every citizen confidently to hold these same beliefs and expectations as realistic and true?

Is this just work for educators or sociologists, for psychologists or economists? Is this work to be undertaken on a band-aid level, as remedial redesign in classrooms and districts or as beneficent but faceless initiatives concocted in boardrooms, think tanks, or propaganda mills?

No. This must be the work of the society as a whole and of its political systems on every level from village to suburb to city to state to federal. It must be the work and the commitment of every leader at every level.

The bullet points above must be part of a manifesto, an educational bill of rights that inspires and commits government to build a system around these principles:

All children must live in physically and emotionally healthy communities and be properly nourished and cared for as a precondition for learning.

Every family must have access to schools that are responsive and committed to the well-being and success of each student, where each student is known, challenged, and supported.

Access to learning and its fruits cannot be not limited by race, income, family situation, faith, gender, or other external or personal factors.

The learning needs of each student must be met in full without detriment to what the student may attain.

Schools and educators must be liberated and encouraged to bring the best of what is known and what might yet be known into every classroom in equal service to every child.

This work is built on hope, hope that may seem wildly idealistic but is fundamental to a just and equitable society.

These expectations and beliefs can only be met when every member of society can see clearly, from cradle to grave, a pathway to a life free from debilitating worry and dispiriting stress, a society in which material and physical security are the rightful and realistic expectation of every citizen.

We must begin by shouting from the rooftops the need for change, and then we must create circumstances and places where educators from all sectors might come together to share ideas, resources, questions, and practices so that every community might attain the same level of confident optimism about the purposes and prospects of education, of going to school.

I don't know how this is going to happen, but it won't until more of us begin to acknowledge not only education's role in sustaining the status quo (pun unintentional but apt) but also to imagine and embrace the role that all schools, public and private, might play together as engines and exemplars of authentic and equitable change.

And to bring this back to the place we are, we might even ask whether the Independent Curriculum Group's foundational Principles of Independent Curriculum, guidelines for equitable, mission-driven teaching and learning, might be a part of this larger manifesto for change.

What do you think?

Not Your Father's School, March 10, 2019

34

FERGUSON: TETHERING OURSELVES TO WHAT MATTERS

A while back I realized that once upon a time I was actually in Ferguson, Missouri.

It was around Christmas of 1970, and I was visiting a friend— in fact a girlfriend—in Florissant, the other town with which Ferguson shared its high school.

Ferguson and Florissant were then, at least as I recall, quick-sprung suburbs of modest tract houses and orderly streets, having grown probably way too rapidly to house manpower for the giant McDonnell-Douglas plant and other factories we drove by on the highway. Ferguson was a poster-child town for American postwar suburbia, a new phenomenon to me on that scale, although I guess I had seen smaller versions around Buffalo.

I vividly remember the moment in which I most egregiously embarrassed myself, asking, as we drove along another long, low brick-and-glass building that I figured must produce airline components by the thousand, "What do they make in there?"

"That's my high school," was the rather chilly response from my soon-to-be ex-girlfriend. And indeed it was McCluer High School, forty-some years later the school of Michael Brown.

I had seen big public high schools before, but nothing on the scale of McCluer. My friend and I had talked about our schools before, naturally, and my eyes had goggled at the number of students in her class—many hundreds, perhaps a thousand—as hers had goggled at the tiny number, seventy or so, in mine. Two Americas, or at least two distinct American experiences, has met. And now I had seen, and passed a kind of unintentional judgment, on a big part of hers.

In those days the American high school as factory was not a metaphor I had yet encountered, and maybe it hadn't been created, but McCluer, from the highway, certainly had that look about it. In 1968 it had sent my friend and a handful of her classmates off to "elite" New England colleges, and one imagines, darkly, that it had also yielded more than its share—there is no such thing as a fair share in this—of students whose names are now etched in the blackish stone of a long, low memorial in Washington, D. C. The civil rights movement was a big thing in our lives, but the signal tragedy of our coming of age was Vietnam.

Like so many other towns on the edges of great cities, Ferguson, barely having caught up with itself as a teeming suburb, was destined for still more change. Its story of white flight, job loss, and tax base erosion is pretty common, and I can only surmise what each of these extended, slow-motion paroxysms must have meant to successive generations of teachers and students at McCluer High School.

I can surmise, but because there are plenty of people who lived and are living it, I have scarcely a right even to try.

And now, perhaps marking an end and a new beginning, we have the tragedy of Michael Brown and the larger tragedy of Ferguson. This is most of all a tragedy for America, a place where change comes so rapidly and seems increasingly untethered from the core values that we claim to hold at the center of our society: in the words of the Superman prologue that any McCluer student of the 1960s could have recited, Truth, Justice, and the American Way.

In 1970 we were learning in Southeast Asia that our nation could no longer, if ever it could have, bend steel in our bare hands or change the course of mighty rivers.

We were developing our special technique for leaping headlong into situations whose implications were obscure and unpredictable, where steel could break and mighty rivers flood. Our suburbs, a kind of point of national pride even as we understood some of the irony of their sameness and sterility (thank you, *Mad Magazine* and John Updike), were ultimately going to be just as unpredictable in their development, and the body of Michael Brown, moldering for so long not in its grave but by the side of the street, seems to symbolize a situation we might have seen coming and done something about long ago.

We just let things happen. We let our high schools look (and some people say feel) like factories, we let our factories look like ruins, we let communities decay into war zones, we let our police forces look like armies. I don't want to think that in all this we have begun to look more and more like our true selves or that it is all beginning to look like our destiny.

Lots of educators these days talk about "mindfulness." Too often this sounds like yoga and aromatherapy, but we need to embrace this notion on a macro level and use the lessons that are staring us in the face in Ferguson and ten thousand other places that haven't erupted but that have been just as caught up in the mindless currents of American social history. Superman isn't here, and I stopped waiting for him after the assassinations of MLK and RFK in '68, so it's going to be up to us and our children (and, surprise! our students) to get us back on a path toward Truth and Justice.

As educators, we have to begin to stand up and name the places where we have gone wrong: income inequality, persistent racism, the dismissal of education itself as a tool for social justice. These are topics we cannot ignore in our classes and in those conversations we call professional development. We in independent schools like to talk about our public purpose, and the biggest public purpose of all is to make sure that our society endures and that it is driven by the better angels of our nature. We need to face up to reality and acknowledge that these angels exist, must exist and be nurtured, and that their urgings must tether us mindfully and heartfully to our values and to one another.

And what would this mean in practice?

For one thing, working to build some transparency around privilege in our own communities. It may be a long way from your campus to Ferguson, but you probably have some students who travel a similar route each day. How much does your school community acknowledge the differences in resources and opportunity that exist with in it, and how often do we ask ourselves and our students to contemplate what these differences in cultural, social, and economic capital mean? How often do we operate under the kind of blasé assumption that we all share a kind of cozy sameness in our lives? Acknowledging the degree to which this is not true is a step toward opening deeper conversations about what these differences mean not just in our own schools and communities but in the world.

For another, we need to make effective and strategic efforts to bring "the real world" into our teaching. If you dig back to the era of the Founding Fathers and some of our earliest schools, you can find plenty of aspirational "mission" language around preparing citizens to live in a democratic society; John Dewey then said it again at greater length. Let's embrace this notion explicitly and stop pretending that daily events have nothing to do with 6th-grade English or 10th-grade Biology or Latin III or Studio Art. They have plenty to do with all of what we teach, and teachers need to see their curricula as preparation for a life in the world and make note of the clear but often complex connections between class content and the social and cultural context of students' lives.

It's not about standing on soapboxes and haranguing students and colleagues to care. It's about realizing that the challenging issues of the world, whether they relate to Ferguson or climate change or global terrorism, have a place in our schools that ought to be making urgent demands our thoughtful, and above all honest, attention.

Not Your Father's School, September 2, 2014

35

A MANDATE FOR HARD WORK

It has to be the greatest headline I've read in a long time: "Election Unleashes a Flood of Hope Worldwide." The _New York Times_ article on the global response to the election of Barack Obama as U.S. president certainly mirrors local reaction among the educators and students where I work.

One of the words I have not heard very often regarding the election, however, is "mandate." A few years back any election that involved a simple plurality was hailed by the victor as a mandate, and yet, in this decisive year, pundits and politicos alike have refrained from its use.

But, idealist that I am, I do believe that this election was a mandate. However, I like to believe that the mandate was not for Barack Obama and his supporters to rule but rather for something deeper, and ultimately far more potent: the election was a mandate for the American people to pull up our socks and start working together to address the challenges that face us.

On the educational front the challenges are clear and the list of failed attempted solutions long. More and more public school children are being left behind as failure and drop-out rates soar, while the teaching of real content is being abandoned in favor of year-long exercises in standardized test preparation as schools scramble to keep their increasingly meager funding and teachers sell their creative pedagogical souls in order to keep their jobs and their tiny raises. Teacher unions are caught between supporting real academic change that teachers know will help their students and defending their members from bad externally imposed initiatives and public attack; in a particularly vicious self-fulfilling prophecy, the more unions are seen as defensive, the more they are regarded as working against the interest of change, and of kids, and the more this seems to become the case.

In a cruel twist that is hardly surprising because it has become an American tradition, it is private and independent school students in more or less unregulated schools who thrive and proceed onward to four-year colleges in numbers vastly disproportionate to the percentage of American students they represent. The reasons for this are clear: not only are students at these schools more consistently (and often heavily) funded, they are often the children of relatively affluent parents whose commitment to and understanding of the educational process is high from the start. As socioeconomic classes have become increasingly stratified in the time of George W. Bush, the gap between the material haves and have-nots has opened into an even greater gap between educational haves and have-nots.

But there are other reasons. As schools of choice, private schools and the subset of independent schools that are usually the intended subject matter of this blog are privileged to allow their teachers to teach as they see fit and to develop strategies for engaging students—and families—in what at their best are true learning communities. Few licensure or standardized testing requirements trouble these schools, and accreditation agencies usually have little trouble giving their imprimatur to their work. Similarly, colleges accept their students in bulk and prospective families (many of whom can pay, but not all—financial aid improves access to many schools even for the poorest families) line up to fill empty seats.

Furthermore, these schools are free to pick and choose from among the best educational practices available. Guided by school-determined missions, their faculties and administrations are free to use any means necessary to serve student bodies they know well both as people and as learners. They need not fear including substantial elements of "character education" or learning focused on civic engagement into their programs, nor do they shy away from considering the arts and even athletic competition as part of a holistic learning experience.

Independent schools are seen as so desirable that "school choice" and voucher activists continue to work for ways to allow public funds to be used toward tuitions at such schools. For many reasons, such schools represent a kind of ideal to many families.

I think that one could argue as to whether freedom from regulation has been a cause or an effect of independent schools' relative success; as long as their students appear to thrive by conventional measures, there is little perceived need to control their work by such unconventional measures as annual testing or Adequate Yearly Progress reports. No one worries whether the science faculty are certified at schools that send their students off to the most selective colleges.

If President Barack Obama and the 111th Congress want to improve America's educational system, it is time to turn away from the failures of No Child Left Behind and the absurdities of hyperregulation. They need to invest the public—eager for real change—and their supporters in the teachers' unions in a program of educational reform that mimics not an industrial, one-size-fits-all model but rather the independent schools that have a proven and sustained record of success.

Along with a return to local control of schools in the context of a real effort to develop curricula that will prepare students for college and the 21st-century workforce, this would mean increasing funding for teacher education programs that support both subject-matter knowledge and real pedagogical and curriculum-development expertise, including finding ways to provide incentives for the most able students to enter these programs; encouraging all schools to create serious, mission-driven professional development programs designed to bring faculties together as communities of practice; looking around the world for model programs that bring families and schools together in the common cause of educating children well; instituting universal pre-school and kindergarten programs that focus on both cultural and pre-textual literacy skills that will prepare all students to read and succeed from early elementary years forward;

abandoning mass-production standardized testing and replacing it with authentic and in-depth assessment that rewards real understanding, real knowledge, and the skills and habits of mind necessary for educational and vocational success in our century;

such assessment would necessarily built by teachers and schools and keyed to educational goals they set, informed by the most current research in education, cognition, and societal needs as well as knowledge of their own students and missions; and making access to college and top-flight pre-professional training available and affordable for all students.

Conservatives should rejoice that these proposals don't even require adding to a federal bureaucracy, although some of them cost money that will probably have to come from a combination of local, state, and federal sources. There's no real need for a department of education here, even, although I think that education is so critical that I can't conceive of the federal government not playing at least a clearing-house and advocacy role in education reform.

I began this blog in my belief in the value of a set of practices that I call the New Progressivism and that have obtained wide currency in independent schools. I believe that these practices, detailed elsewhere but implicit in the policy recommendations listed above, can save American education and American children, even in the lowest-performing schools.

The election should give heart not only to educators, but also to students, families, and citizens at large, but we need to recognize that the mandate is for all of us to embrace new and not-so-new ideas that can really bring change. I have presented a few of these, and, difficult as they might be to implement, I think that they could truly help make the kind of difference for which so many of us voted and that so many around the nation and around the world have been craving.

The New Progressivism, November 5, 2008

36

IDEALISM, CONSTRAINTS, AND YOU. STAND UP FOR WHAT YOU KNOW IS RIGHT!

Idealism has fueled the Independent Curriculum Group since our founding. We envisioned a better kind of educational system, one driven not by standardized testing requirements, the profit motive, or powerful anxieties about things like college admission and institutional prestige.

Above all we envisioned education not as one monolithic structure framed and maintained by giant corporate interests but rather as a highly complex ecosystem in which factors like student interests and needs and institutional beliefs and values would underlie a system designed and operated to produce not just engaged and active global citizens or life-long learners—to pick on the often tired-sounding language of many school mission statements—but curious and competent denizens of a better, more just, more hospitable world. The key, to the ICG, would be each school's ability to identify the very best in its foundations and aspirations and then to embody its value system in an idiosyncratic learning environment and set of learning experiences reflective of its core beliefs.

We have our own ideas of what this might look like, and I imagine that many readers share the broad outlines of our idealistic vision. But we don't have a prescription, and we no more believe that there is one best way to educate than that there is one and only one right answer to the question, "What is Hamlet about?"

Whenever I am contacted by a school with a question about "curriculum," in whatever sense, I go immediately to the school's statements of values and beliefs. I burrow into the mission statement, the core values, the board statement of diversity, the tagline, and even the motto, seeking the common threads that might be pulled tight and highlighted to help the school identify its own "convictions" and then to find the courage to live them, even if living them somehow repudiates aspects of its "business as usual" policies and programs.

These fruits of my excavations can sometimes feel a bit pat and glib, at other times too clever by half. "Lifelong learning" and "global citizenship" may invite cheap shots because of their frequent appearances in mission statements, but if a school takes the time not only to define these but to embed them as desirable values into its programs, it's making the world a better place. Taglines can be cute and mottos cuter, but if a school really tries to imagine and build their meanings into the experience of students (and families), then the efforts of whoever chose or created these are yielding something greater than just some obscure Latin on a seal or an eye-catching slogan on a landing page.

With the exception of those places that occasionally throw mottos in the faces of their students as behavioral correctives (to wonderful ends sometimes, we happily admit), how many schools have regular and serious discussions of their own ideals and how these might—and must, we think—inform the development of policies and programs? How many department meetings start with the mission statement to drive conversations about not just course offerings but even assessment and the evaluation of student work?

This is not just an independent school conversation. Public school systems have their own mission statements and other proclamations of aspirations, and we cannot forget that public education is on a profound and urgent quest for a "positive social good" whose beneficiaries are every child and every being. Warped and distracted as public schools and their leaders may seem under the scrutiny of the media and political critics, public schools must truly be all things to all people. And they must first and foremost represent the highest ideals for community membership and the living of active, empathetic, and productive lives in the community. (If you're in an independent, private, or charter school with a narrowly defined mission, try imagining how your school would go about educating every student in your community!)

I've always like the idea behind the Mao quote, "Let a hundred flowers bloom!" Allowing a multiplicity of ideas and ideals to take root, and then to bloom, is what the ICG has had in mind, too. We know that for every blossoming ideal there are countervailing constraints thrown up by the "real world," but we know that ideals are worth fighting for.

Ideals worth fighting for can't just be words on a page or a website, vapid truisms used to make people feel better. These words—missions, pillars, standards, whatever—must be the subject of ongoing exegesis and analysis, like the words of a sacred text. Which, in fact, is exactly what they are, in their way.

Maybe your founders just hired some graphic artist to design the seal, or maybe a consultant marched the board through a mission-statement "exercise" to appease accreditors. Maybe those "core standards" are just intended as feel-goods for prospective families. Maybe that board "diversity statement," however well intended by its creators, is really only regarded as another box, checked. Is this the best you can be? Is this what you wanted from a school and from a career when you became an educator? Boxes checked, feel-goods, appeasement? Is this what you believe in when the kids walk in?

Yes, yes, the constraints. But those constraints, whether they look like financial sustainability or imperatives around "preparation," are only constraints, and they do not have to be prison walls for ideals. Can a student be well prepared for Ivy University and at the same time have had a school experience that that has supported in every way their becoming a truly wonderful person with a probing mind and a heart as big as the world? Cannot a school be full and thriving without its programs damping the passions or crushing the curiosity of its students en route to the instrumental outcomes craved by families?

I often make the point that Advanced Placement courses, often seen as soul-crushing and an early ICG bugbear, can be taught as vibrant, engaging, and mission-aligned experiences that yield both passing scores and excited students. Teachers who can pull this off know how to work around constraints in the service of their hopes and dreams as teachers. They know that constraints do not have to be a dead hand on passionate learning.

Where does your school stand on this? How often does your community interrogate its foundational and aspirational words in search of guidance toward more effective and heartful programming? And how can you help it key its actions to its ideals?

The Independent Curriculum Blog, February 6, 2019

37

END BORDER CHILD SEPARATION AND INCARCERATION NOW! SILENCE IS COMPLICITY

What does it take to remind a society of its responsibility toward children? Or maybe it's that societies don't really see their responsibilities toward children in the same sentimental terms in which parents see theirs. Every politician wants to be seen kissing babies (a trope that was nearly obsolete until revived by the current Incarcerator-in-Chief), but very many fewer of these politicos seem eager to stand up for children's education, health and well-being, or apparently even their human right to be with their own families.

The current situation at the United States border with Mexico cannot stand. Soon enough we can expect to see concentration camps for separated parents and children elsewhere in our nation, and we know it. We can name this is an unimaginable evil, yet we can imagine it and cannot act to stop it.

There are those who will throw support for a woman's right to choose what happens to her own body, including terminating an unwanted pregnancy, right back at those of us who decry border separation and incarceration. Nobody thinks abortion is a wonderful option, but many of those same people are also supportive of restrictions on the availability of affordable birth control. These are as much about the long-term health and welfare of children yet unborn as they are about s-e-x. If you say that because you disapprove of something else that this makes it okay to wrest crying children from their parents and lock them up, whether in cages or at a Walmart, you missed some important lessons and discussions in your moral education. (If you style yourself an observant Christian, maybe your Bible can help; try Matthew 18.)

The Interested Child calls on every elected and appointed official in the United States, at all levels, to denounce the policy of forced separation and child incarceration at our borders and to act decisively through federal, state, and local action to end this policy. (State action? you ask. Whose National Guard units comprise the enforcement infrastructure? Your state's?)

The Interested Child, June 19, 2018

38

ALLIES: SCHOOLS MUST SPEAK <u>WITH</u> THE KIDS—NOT JUST FOR THEM!

It's been an appalling few weeks and an appalling year. The sickening "Varsity Blues" scandal bookends the forced separation of families at the U. S. border and the continuing, tragic fallout from Sandy Hook and Parkland. More hyperselective colleges than ever admitted fewer than 10% of their applicants this year, functionally turning "offices of undergraduate admission" into offices of rejection, despite all the warmth and reassurances that school-based college counselors and Frank Bruni can give applicants. And every single school I hear from has students out of school on stress-related medical leave.

You're likely reading this as an educator, and your heart is aching along with mine, I know. Figuratively or for real, the little "Ally" sticker on your door is there for every kid, regardless of demographic particulars. This I believe.

But what is your school or organization doing to be an ally? What institutional steps has your board, administration, and faculty collectively taken to actively support not only its own students but all children in the struggle for a secure, healthy, and equitable future?

We've seen the "Parkland Kids" and a mobilized generation stand up and fight for rational gun laws, but too often the public response has been to admire the students' courage and maturity rather than actually to engage with their life-and-death issue. What could schools as institutions do to further this cause, which belongs not just to the survivors but to all of us?

Last month around the world students walked out of class to raise awareness of global climate change. Is removing disciplinary consequences from such principled and urgent acts the best we can do to support these students on this apocalyptic issue? The kids, in so many ways, are trying to teach ALL OF US lessons that their schools should be taking up as far more pressing than just checking boxes on college applications.

The National Association of Independent Schools persists in advising schools against having students serve as trustees (see HERE), stating that "their general maturity can make it difficult for them to move beyond their particular experiences as current students." Does anyone who works with high schoolers or who watched the student-organized pro-gun control rallies across the country last year believe that kids are categorically beyond being responsible board members? I, for one, think the NAIS position is shameful, and I applaud schools that give students a voice in governance.

Every educator knows that the college admission system is broken, and we know that much of the blame rests with a self-serving and amorphous industry in which testing giants, rankings publications, and test-prep and application support counselors make billions off the anxiety of parents and students. Some schools have found ways to band together to reject and repudiate the injustices and to propose alternatives—the Independent Curriculum Group and the Mastery Transcript Consortium are two, and groups like Challenge Success, the Education Conservancy, and Making Caring Common are a few more—but most schools do not seem to prioritize this work. Perhaps they fear that gradeless transcripts or too much "caring" will weaken their brands and their appeal to prospective families, but doesn't inaction amount to complicity in a system based on winners and losers that harms kids—and turns some parents into grotesque headliners in the Varsity Blues affair?

We have an equity issue in our K–12 education system as a whole, with uneven funding and self-enforced separation among the professional cohorts of public, public charter, general private, and independent school educators. We all of us, no matter where we teach or work, care about the success of all kids. Why, then, can't we unite in a common effort not only to bring equity to the system but also to converse and teach and learn from one another as educators? Individuals can cross sector boundaries by going to conferences and EdCamps, but what initiatives can SCHOOLS undertake to build inter-sector bridges in a shared commitment to a better future for every child?

Thank you for being, through your interest in something like the Independent Curriculum Group, an ally of students in the work of creating better learning experiences for them. Now, perhaps, it's time for all of us to exhort our schools and communities to get together, stand up, and apply the collective power of our *institutions* to doing the things that every news cycle reminds us must be done to save our children, our planet—and our schools.

It's time for individual allies to mobilize our schools to speak with our students. We know, as the kids do, what needs to be said. Let's start saying it together.

The Independent Curriculum Blog, February 6, 2019

39

CARNEGIE'S LIBRARIES AND THE COLLEGE–ANXIETY CABAL: WOULD TREATING AND SUPPORTING EQUITABLE COLLEGE ACCESS AS A PUBLIC GOOD CHANGE THE NATIONAL CONVERSATION ON COLLEGE ADMISSION?

Like most educators, I have been reading this week of the admission-bribery and test-cheating scandal that has ensnared both wealthy parents and a small host of venal rats—coaches, so-called college advisors, and even school-based test administrators—who have been living off their twisted ambitions. Of course I have wanted to throw up, when I wasn't wanting to just sit and weep. But maybe, in all this, there is a way forward.

The real issue is not rich people being jerks or how they enlist compliant abettors to help them defile the moral and social contract. Back when kids had to study Roman history, a primary lesson was that the wealthy and powerful have always been able to find loopholes—side doors, I guess we are calling them now—that allow some of them and their accomplices to situate themselves outside the frameworks of law, decency, and equity. What else is new?

The issue is that college admissions has become far more than a matter of getting into some college. College rankings are not only a multi-million-dollar industry in their own right but the engine—and one thinks this is increasingly by design—of a College–Anxiety Cabal that uses fear and envy to drive a multi-billion-dollar industry in which standardized test preparation and application support have become the norm in every middle-class (or higher) community and are regarded as absolute necessities in every public and private high school where shoe-horning a significant portion of graduates into selective four-year colleges is the expectation. Add to this the billions more that stressed and frightened families pay to make sure that their children are engaged in résumé-burnishing activities from outside-of-school sports to arts lessons to pricey "service learning" activities and travel.

Grooming a child for the highest levels of competition in this sick beauty pageant—the quest for admission to prestigious colleges that may accept fewer than ten percent of their applicants—takes a vast toll in time, money, and psychic energy and well-being. It's no wonder that the suicide and mental health treatment levels for kids in this rarefied world are soaring. It's no wonder that kids crack ethically under the strain—ask administrators in these schools about academic dishonesty rates—and that parents and guardians do, too.

Well, news from the College–Anxiety Cabal sells newspapers, as they say, and we saw this week, when evidence of bad behavior among "elites" has been splashed all over our screens, that news of rot in the system REALLY, REALLY sells. When even the BBC leads with a scandal in American college admissions, you know that the media money machine is whirring.

Wealthy schools can offer their students more support in the college search–apply–choose process, in the form of knowledgeable personal counseling, than poorer schools can. And even in affluent communities, counseling caseloads diverge dramatically between private and public high schools. The issue, to go back to my initial point, is not about bad rich people, but about access to the kinds of wise and caring support that can help each student put their best foot forward in the quest for a post-secondary experience that will serve, challenge, and satisfy them while preparing them for lives of meaning and purpose. Wealthier kids in wealthier communities simply have more access to this kind of support, which has warped an already imperfect system in further favor of kids with money.

It's worth reminding ourselves that we have a few things in our world for which we ought to thank the rich. It's not about trickle-down economics—that's a myth as bogus as the Tooth Fairy. It's about institution-building. And one of these institutions might provide a model for a path forward.

In the center of hundreds of towns across America today there sits a Carnegie Library. Once upon a time, the richest man in the world set himself to giving away the bulk of his fortune, and he valued education and reading. Through foundation grants, he put tens of millions of circa-1900 dollars into giving communities places where residents could have free access to the latest in books and periodicals. Sure, some of these libraries are bigger and fancier than others (Carnegie required participation in these projects from local communities and governments), but there they are. Often understaffed and underfunded in 2019, public libraries, whether "Carnegie" or not, represent a long-ago dream of "intellectual equity" and access for all to ideas and learning. This dream needs to be revisited and revitalized.

What if every community had, as a service offered through its public library or public library system, a college and career advising office? I can envision such an office tucked into the back of the building, staffed by a knowledgeable counselor or counselors with experience or certification, ready to support any child in the community in exploring post-secondary options and preparing applications. "Which schools should I apply to?" and the timeline for standardized testing would become just pieces of a plan worked out by every interested student and family, guided by an expert.

Larger communities would need more of these counselors-at-large, and they would need to be paid. Focused on post-secondary, they wouldn't actually be duplicating the efforts of public school guidance officers, whose brief is far broader (which makes their college counseling role even more challenging, on top of caseloads typically in the hundreds). These counselors-at-large would need to be on the job full time, and they would need access to the kinds of digital tools available now to school-based counselors.

In the meantime, their office spaces in public libraries would by definition offer internet access and reference collections where any student, parent, or guardian could do research on post-secondary options, colleges, and the college search–apply–choose process.

Could some rich person, a modern-day Carnegie, fund this kind of student support system to all communities? Possibly, and it would be a full-on public good were such a person to do so. I invite all these billionaires obsessed with college admission to start their gift planning.

But why should this enterprise be left in private, eleemosynary hands? Access to higher education is a PUBLIC good, and why should not each community make its own regular and ongoing investment in ensuring that each child be afforded the kind of counseling that is today reserved for the affluent? If post-secondary education for all is a goal, why should not each child be given every opportunity to attain what is appropriate and best for them?

Andrew Carnegie built the libraries, but from the beginning their staffing and maintenance has been regarded and supported (sometimes deficiently, alas) as a public enterprise for the benefit of the entire community. The provision of community counselors-at-large should be regarded as just such a public good.

Just as a kind of footnote, the greatest challenge for many families in the whole college admission "thing" is financial aid: how it works and how to obtain it.

There has to be a better system for helping families with this than overworked school counselors or for-pay services. In Massachusetts, the state's Educational Financing Authority willingly provides expertise to schools and individuals, but probably too few people know about this. By expanding the

Authority's outreach programs, what MEFA "knows" could be shared with more of the people who need to know it. Boosting the budget at the state level for such bodies (and establishing them where they don't yet exist) would make critical expertise available, again as a public good and public service.

Yes, rich people and an inequitable process have fouled the waters of college admission, but providing for every child as a public service what the affluent now pay billions for would cast a spotlight on the need to re-envision and reform the entire system. What now looks to so many like a "corrupt" process, calling into question the very integrity and value of the most prized colleges, might yet become a more regularized and transparent process in which every citizen, rich or poor, has an important stake.

And as always in education, these stakes are high: nothing less than a future of learning and individual attainment in a context of equity and justice.

The Independent Curriculum Blog, March 14, 2019

40

RAISING OUR VOICES AGAINST GUN VIOLENCE

I have written elsewhere about the <u>horrific ways in which children have been treated in the world</u> and about <u>my cousin's work as a grief counselor in the aftermath of the massacre in her hometown of Sandy Hook, Connecticut</u>. But the world seems to have gone even crazier in the past couple of years, and the shooting at the Marjory Stoneman Douglas High School in Florida last week was just one more episode of madness too much. And I'm not talking just about the shooter, but about the studied way in which politicians keep sidestepping the issue of gun violence and gun control.

If you're reading this you care about kids. You are likely a parent or a guardian or an educator. You watch kids every day. You have probably been watching the Olympics and marveling at the teenagers on skis and snowboards, for example, hurling themselves into the air, spinning crazily, and landing in the medal zone. You know that these are passionately interested children, and you pray that the sports systems that have brought them to Pyeong Chang are healthier and less exploitative than what we have been hearing about in women's gymnastics. But I suppose we all wonder.

What we know about mass shootings is that nothing will happen, or at least that nothing has happened yet. Politicians bray about "thoughts and prayers," mumble something about "mental health," and then go back and curl up at the feet of their gun-lobby masters, apparently content that the cycle of violence is now as American as apple pie and that re-election is in their money-filled bag.

Some kids have even learned to capitalize on the sick pointlessness of all this, and the cycle now includes copy-cat threats to schools, replacing false fire alarms as an effective way to get attention, have some lulz, and maybe even delay that algebra test for a day. Someone, somewhere is keeping a tally, but Thursday and Friday's toll of these was well into the dozens, nationally, by my quick review of local news sites across the country. And apparently a few of the thwarted threats were for real. Jesus wept.

But the children are speaking up in positive ways, too, and the media, at least, are suddenly beginning to listen. I read in my local paper today a story about a rally held by Parkland, Florida, students in which they spoke out—loud and proud and passionate and angry—on the issue of guns. "We call B–S!" was their cry. Bravo! Is ours.

And we have calls to action from other places: Other organizations are proposing days for student and teacher walk-outs and teach-ins. The idea is to spark enough positive action to capture enough of the attention of the voting public to, in turn, capture the attention of politicians at all levels—hopefully enough attention to drown out the gun lobby's mandate for inaction.

The Interested Child supports these and other efforts to curb the United States's appalling rate of gun violence: on an average day, 96 people die by the gun, including seven children and teens. This is unacceptable.

And if children's voices can help in this effort, we urge our readers to engage themselves and their own interested children in this work. This is not about exploiting children for political gain but about somehow finding the right combination of voices and messages to change the world, or at least our little part of it.

I don't even understand why this is about politics at all. Who can disagree that kids' lives should be protected by the adults who write and enforce the laws of the land?

The Interested Child, February 19, 2018

HERE ON EARTH: EDUCATION FOR A STRUGGLING PLANET

Each new scientific report seems to shorten the time to the horizon over which our planet will plunge into climate catastrophe, and the endless wars that began before many of our students were born seem to keep metastasizing across the surface of the earth. As educators it may be too late for us to resolve these crises, but we have to give our students at least a fighting chance.

Educators keen on the cross-cultural understanding aspects of "global education" and the gleeful entrepreneurs who imagine a world of markets without boundaries are all excited about what schools can do help bring about these visions, and I'm sympathetic at least with the former and would like to think of the latter as at least plausible if it could be achieved equitably. Equally excited for all the right reasons are the "environmental ed" teachers and other Green advocates working to make schools more environmentally conscious and responsible and to help their students develop eco-friendly attitudes and skills.

For the purposes of imagining a generally better, safe, more peaceful world, I lump together these perspectives in the essays that follow. I'm growing old in this world, but I have grandchildren, and I want our schools to be doing all that they can to make this world a whole lot better when today's babies are grown up.

41

UN-SUSTAINABILITY?

The headline in *The Chronicle of Higher Education* says it all, but unfortunately the article says even more: that among the early victims of the financial crisis as it plays out on college campuses are likely to be schools' sustainability efforts. What for many schools has been discretionary spending— "slushy," as one college sustainability officer quoted in the article describes the funding for her job—will be curtailed as smaller colleges focus more tightly on services deemed essential.

The public's attention seems at last to have been brought to the idea that environmental sustainability is a survival issue, and forward thinkers in the education community have begun to articulate a comprehensive, integrated vision of sustainability as a strategic educational direction. It's lamentable, and possibly more, that the immediacies of faculty salaries and plant maintenance may limit or put an end to what some colleges are trying to do, just at what looks so much like the ideal "teachable moment."

New Progressivist schools at the primary and secondary levels have taken a range of approaches to the issue of sustainability, from whole-hog commitment to environmental studies, environmental action, and campus sustainability to more measured, curriculum-focused efforts to teach students the complex interrelationships between the human and natural environments, the economy, social structures, and even the arts. The common element is the desire to help students develop an awareness of the impact of their own lives—and vice versa—on the places and cultural milieus in which they live.

Among the more sophisticated approaches to issues of sustainability is "place-based education," in which Tip

O'Neill's adage that "all politics are local" is extended to a deep understanding of the way historical and natural forces have converged to shape specific communities. An intensive study of a single city block or rural stream can yield extraordinary amounts of information about the way people have lived, the ways they have regarded their environments, and the ways in which stewardship for place might yet lead us out of our political, social, economic, and climatic thickets.

Rather than let operational sustainability efforts peter out in our educational institutions, I like to think that progressive educators will see the current crisis as little short of a mandate to guide students in digging even deeper into what has made aspects of our society so patently un-sustainable; this may seem re-active, but the work has already been started and needs only to be expanded and supported. Through place-based education, through the incorporation of issues of social justice and economic theory into our curricula, and through an optimistic commitment to sustainability as a mantra for building a better world, let us work as educators to keep the concept alive and well.

We invite readers to share with us the ways that schools are approaching this topic.

The New Progressivism, October 9, 2008

42

PUBLIC PURPOSE: ENVIRONMENTALISM IN INDEPENDENT SCHOOLS—AND OTHERS!

I'm not a knowledgeable environmentalist—certainly no expert—but, like many of us, I do what I can to live a greener life. I'm also a big fan of getting kids outdoors as part of their education. All of this sparks my interest in what schools can do and are doing to facilitate these goals.

In 2005 I attended a conference at the Lawrenceville School in New Jersey with a focus on environmental sustainability in all aspects of schools' lives and programs. Part of the program was a focus on the then-pretty-new Island School, one of the term-away programs of which I wrote earlier and the brainchild of some Lawrenceville folks.

I met some very smart and interesting people at this event, and I heard some compelling presentations. But the biggest thing that I took away was that a couple of the independent schools in attendance had appointed what amounted to Chief Sustainability Officers.

One of these, the-then CSO of Lawrenceville, Josh Hahn, reviewed their portfolio: reducing energy and resource use, sourcing Green and local products and materials, being an administration-level voice in policy and planning discussions, and supporting (and providing some of) his school's educational efforts around environmental sustainability. Pretty cool stuff!

We know I'm a cockeyed idealist, so it might not surprise you that this idea seemed like the greatest thing since sliced bread. These couple of schools had elevated the environmental voice—often heard here and there in schools in what can feel like nagging tones—from gadfly to guru. They had put real authority in the hands of someone who could continue expanding expertise in an evolving field even as they helped the school with operational and strategic issues at the cabinet level.

At my school at this time we were still struggling with simple recycling (town regulations seemed to be at issue), and our environmental initiatives came largely from a few very enthusiastic teachers and an outdoorsman CFO. Clearly the Chief Sustainability Officer concept was not going to work for every school—not, then, for ours—for a whole lot of reasons.

But some quick math suggested to me that on a large, multi-building residential campus—like Lawrenceville's—such a position could soon pay for itself. It was in fact among such schools that the [now-departed—PG] Green Cup Challenge came to be. The challenge had been born as an inter-dormitory competition at Phillips Exeter Academy "as a campus-wide energy conservation competition designed to raise awareness about energy consumption" and went interscholastic—we independent schools do like rivalries—in 2005–06, with something over a half-dozen schools competing. In 2012–13 over 300 schools from all sectors participated, saving, according to reports some 1.5 gigawatt-hours of electricity.

It turns out, of course, that not just big boarding schools need to save energy and focus on environmental sustainability. In 2007, responding to a challenge put forth by New York mayor Michael Bloomberg, a group of schools came together to form the Green Schools Alliance, which now has about 3000 member schools worldwide, private and public; the Alliance now sponsors the Green Cup Challenge, now expanded to include several different kinds of competitions.

A number of big boarding schools do bring great resources as well as economies of scale to the work of environmental sustainability. Berkshire School in Massachusetts has built an enormous solar array—largest in the state—and Connecticut's Hotchkiss School (where Josh Hahn is now the Assistant Head of School and Director of Environmental Initiatives) has committed itself "to becoming a carbon-neutral campus by 2020."

In June of this year a group of environmentally concerned educators gathered on the Hotchkiss campus for the National Association of Independent Schools–The Hotchkiss School Summit on Environmental Sustainability in Independent Schools. It was eight years on from the conference I attended at Lawrenceville, and this event gave evidence that the sophistication with which schools are looking at the challenges and opportunities of environmental sustainability has grown as much as the number of independent schools that are getting serious about the issue.

I've referred here on several occasions to the old(ish) chestnut about "private schools with a public purpose." It strikes me that environmental sustainability has become an area in which independent schools are pushing this envelope, from Berkshire's mighty array to Hotchkiss's vast biomass facility to smaller examples like Darrow School's "Living Machine" water treatment facility and leadership in Hudson River Valley environmental education to the place-driven schoolyard-to-table program at the tiny North Country School in New York's Adirondack Mountains. All of these model a path toward environmental awareness and sustainable practice that ought to be having a powerful influence on public policy, from education and energy to zoning laws.

It may be that independent schools are just beginning to find their real voice for expressing their public purpose—the real work, as partners and working exemplars, of turning their resources and their ideas to aims beyond the education of their own students. I'd like to believe that the best of schools' environmental work, as it has spread through the Green Schools Alliance and through the examples and outreach of schools like Darrow and others, may just be the sound of public purpose clearing its throat.

"Independent Schools, Common Perspectives," *Education Week*, August 9, 2013

43

COUNTRY DAY SCHOOLS REDIVIVUS?

It's summertime, and at least in places not subject to air quality warnings, flash flood watches, and severe heat advisories (most of the U.S. this past weekend, I realize), the historical view of American society says kids should be playing outside.

The reality, however, tends to be a little different. It's an indoor kind of world, mostly, and it's no wonder Richard Louv writes about "Nature-Deficit Disorder." It's no wonder some of the most urgent-sounding email I receive comes from the Children & Nature Network, dedicated to creating "world where every child can play, learn and grow in nature."

Two of the schools I've worked in have had "country day school" as part of their names—reflecting a movement, at the turn of the 20th century, to get middle class kids out of their indoor lifestyles and give them, as a part of every day, plenty of exposure to fresh, unpolluted air, pure sunlight, and morally salubrious greenery.

Nowadays, of course, my 90+-year-old country day schools are both embedded deep in suburbia, situated on busy four-lane streets a short walk from shopping malls; so much for "country."

Fortunately, required athletics and felicitous architecture still mean some contact with the out-of-doors and bright sunlight. But these are no longer educational goals in themselves; whatever country day schools once were, mine are no longer in the original sense. And we keep reading about all kinds of schools scrapping outdoor recess to make time for test preparation.

The word of the moment is "innovation," with all of its connotations of technological wizardry and entrepreneurialism. On the plus side, this includes social entrepreneurship, but its domestic version tends to involve doing good mainly in urban, underresourced communities. (Only in its international form does this work seem to reach much beyond cities; school service trip planners do love rural villages.)

Another new trend in education is design thinking—a kind of amped-up, project-based collaborative learning that combines creativity (good) with technical thinking (good), usually in quest of solutions to problems of social significance (good). It's all good, indeed—but in much of its application it has little to do with the Great Outdoors and the kinds of independent learning that kids can do wandering in the woods or paddling down a stream.

Even in independent schools, bastions of the liberal arts, there is an inescapable sense these days that school is about vocational or at least entrepreneurial preparation. Kids at St. Grottlesex may not be studying auto repair, but schools are happy to point out that their college prep curricula are replete with training in the 21st-century "soft skills" that employers are said to crave.

Once upon a time these soft skills—collaboration, creative problem-solving, stick-to-it-iveness (once again, as it we did a century ago, we're calling it grit), and optimism—were the province of either self-teaching (kids playing Robin Hood in the woods or the alleyways) or structured programs like scouting; at the heart of both was the idea of adventure. A hundred years ago a popular literary genre—the series book—featured small groups of like-minded youth (for example, the Motor Maids, the Radio Boys, the Banner Boy Scouts, the Girl Aviators) having really exciting adventures while busily solving all kinds of serious problems—many of them of a highly technical nature, and many of them very much to be tackled in the open air.

(Time here for an acknowledgment that the "structured programs like scouting" and the determinedly bourgeois series books—in particular—were also sometimes vectors for the transmission for attitudes about class and race that in time turned the phrase "white middle class" into an epithet; the Boy Scouts still seem to be struggling to find a way out of some of their early prejudices. But one can perhaps look to this heritage to explain why environmentalism is viewed as elitist in some quarters.)

I'm not sure I see an answer, or even a very clear way ahead, but I wish that more educational gurus could take a real look outside the schoolhouse. This has to go beyond the "outdoor ed centers" to which we sometimes pack kids off for a week during the school year; noble as their aims may be; often their "no-this-or-that!" rules and occasionally overzealous staff members inadvertently present nature as a place of hardship and deprivation—not just a place for what Theodore Roosevelt called, in a very positive sense, "The Strenuous Life."

Design thinking, collaboration, problem-solving, and creativity can all be taught and take place in contexts that keep the door open between the schoolhouse, the home, and the natural world. Today's good ideas are just as applicable to learning in a world defined by the natural environment as they are to learning that happens indoors or online. We have only to turn our serious and concerted attention to the question of "nature-deficit disorder," and we could make easy strides toward erasing it.

It would be interesting to imagine what a return to the original idea of the country day school might look like: mandatory time out of doors, authentic field work. It seems to me that as social issues inequities like rural poverty, the beleaguered family farm, and environmental racism are plenty brutal enough to warrant schools' attention. And bring the laptops! Problems like these can absorb all the online research as well as all the creative thinking kids can do.

The new country day school, or the old country day school with a reinvigorated sense of its purpose as such, might just be as revolutionary in reconnecting kids with nature as their originals were in keeping kids who might otherwise have been undone by the novel luxuries of the early 20th century grounded and healthy by dint of fresh air and sunlight. The reconstituted country day could open kids' eyes to new relationships, not just with nature but with their society and themselves. It would be a satisfyingly modern sort of education, all 21st-century and deeply informed by critical issues.

This new education might even lead to an updated and righteous run of series books; I'd like to think that kids could still be inspired by really multicultural, high-tech, high-drama stories of *The Nanotech Girls in the North Woods*, *The FabLab Rangers on the Mississippi*, or *The Maker Kids and Their Solar Soil Rejuvenator*, wouldn't you? Kids could even read 'em on their smartphones.

"Independent Schools, Common Perspectives," *Education Week*, July 1, 2013

44

EDUCATIONAL INEQUITY: TRYING FOR A GLOBALIZED PERSPECTIVE

Getting an education on this planet is no easy matter. Despite my cautious optimism about the state of affairs in the U.S. after enjoying an instructive Fourth of July parade last week, the news in other parts of the world is often nothing short of appalling.

To wit:

According to the *New York Times*, Roma children in the Czech Republic are vastly and suspiciously overrepresented in that country's "special ed" system—a situation that smacks of segregation and seems to focus on the Romas' "otherness" and long-time social exclusion, to perpetuate an especially pernicious, opportunity-denying underclass status for these kids. Earlier this year the *Times* published a similar report on the status of Slovakia's elementary-age Roma.

In northeastern Nigeria, members of an Islamic extremist group whose name, Boko Haram, translates roughly as "Western education is sacrilege," are thought to be behind a night-time assault on a boarding school that ended in the shooting or burning deaths of at least 22 students. This is the latest and worst in a series of such attacks aimed at deterring parents and children from attending state-sponsored schools.

In other parts of the world stories of violence aimed at keeping children, and especially girls, from an education are increasingly commonplace. The world groaned in frustrated outrage last year when then-14-year-old Malala Yousafzai, an advocate for girls' education in Pakistan, was shot by the Taliban, although no perpetrator has yet been brought to justice.

Crazily, there is often some state or at least political "purpose" to these depredations, and from our transoceanic perspective we can see and deplore them as representative (or worse, stereotypical) ills of whole societies, assigning blame and at least imagining in our readerly minds some policies that might bring them to an end.

These stories satisfy a kind of crude geopolitical logic that is necessarily absent, for all but the most cynical of us, from our frustrated analysis of periodic slaughters of the innocents carried out by maniacs. Better gun laws might help, we know, but in our hearts we fear that madness knows no bounds and is likely to have its cruel way.

But I couldn't help reading the stories of the Roma children and thinking of things much closer to home, of schools and schoolchildren assigned to a kind of perpetual underperformance by uneven funding of schools and even more by the growing economic and educational inequality in U.S. society. We think we have passed well beyond the era of state intentionality behind inequities in the educational system, and we can proudly point to decades of programmatic attempts to close the racial and socioeconomic achievement gap. We can even point to some progress.

Yet the gap persists, in multiple manifestations, and I wonder how a Czech journalist might go about reviewing a comprehensive and data-based report on the variegated American educational landscape like that presented by Uri Treisman at this year's the National Council of Teachers of Mathematics annual conference (click here for links and commentary) earlier this year. Would a Czech investigative reporter, looking at numbers showing a disproportion of low achievement at the lowest ends of the American socioeconomic spectrum, discern a government "war on the poor"? Would he or she see a kind of state intention behind the numbers, a systematic management of the economically disadvantaged designed to keep them that way? Add the rates of incarceration and violence that often parallel the educational statistics for underresourced communities, and some very bitter conclusions might be drawn.

I'm not cynical enough to suggest that this is so, and no doubt some readers are limbering up their fingers to point out that the independent school world from which I come could be seen as an arm of such a disadvantaging system. I can only respond that most of these schools work pretty hard to attract and support students from the lowest rungs of the socioeconomic ladder (you may as well see the numbers here) and to take seriously their putative role as agents of social change on an individual level.

I'd also put forward the rapidly expanding work that independent schools are doing to engage with their communities and in particular with their local public school systems to improve education for all students. (For example, there's the National Network of Schools in Partnership, an exemplary organization supporting this work.) No, it's not much in the great scale of things, but we're a tiny slice of the entire pre-college spectrum. Can we do more? Of course, and schools are working at it.

As an educator, a parent, and a human being, I'm sickened by the ways in which children around the world are made pawns in political and cultural battles. Headlines like those about of Malala Yousafzai or the Nigerian boarding schools make me weep, and reports like those on the Roma infuriate me. But when I go through the exercise of trying to "globalize" my own perspective, I see plenty of things at home to inspire tears and anger. If as a nation we're beginning to make progress in these, then we still have a very long way to go.

"Independent Schools, Common Perspectives," *Education Week,* July 8, 2013

NARRATIVES AND NONSENSE

From time to time the independent school world is swept by some new and trendy idea, and in a very short time some of these ideas seem to be vying to become the controlling narratives or even beacons of salvation. At times we let these ideas become truths, or truisms, that suddenly pop up as conference themes or imperatives for practice or policy. I know that I have been swept along on occasion.

The essays below were written to largely clarify my own thinking on a few "hot" ideas—at least to shake out of them what might be true and real—and to interrogate these trendy tropes for hidden, missing, or downright pernicious elements.

45

DATA ARE PEOPLE, TOO

We keep hearing about data, and how data analysis is going to help education chart its own course toward salvation. I've been swimming in a sea of data lately, trying to make out some landmarks.

When the accrediting process for independent schools added a kind of data requirement a couple of years back, a real one this time, there was an expectation that schools, seeing where the bus was going, would merrily hop aboard. Most schools already had some measurement tools in place—ERB scores, admission tests, PSAT and other college-admission testing records—and so it was just a matter of making some correlations and seeing what changes, to the math program or the English curriculum, were going to be needed. Easy-peasy.

Shortly after this change to the accreditation standards, I did a project for the National Association of Independent Schools on the processes schools were using to go about their data-informed decision-making, and the results were a little surprising. Schools had the data, mostly, but very few had any idea what to do with it or how to create protocols for analyzing it or applying the results. Apparently, with all the proliferation in new kinds of administrative positions, schools had forgotten to sign on their data analysts or institutional researchers. Except in rare cases, few schools looked closely even at their ERB or PSAT scores as reflections of their programs.

NAIS has been working to help schools build the infrastructure and the capacity to use data to understand themselves better. Much of this work has been done on the business side, with dashboards and even bigger data sets to show for their efforts.

Me, I've been trying to figure out what use to make of things like SSAT and ISEE scores, breaking down my school's admission testing data into all kinds of categories and permutations. The SSAT helpfully offers projected SAT scores, so I've looking at how those work out (considering they prognosticate in score bands of 50 to 140 points, it's hard to know the value, exactly) and then how incoming students' percentile scores (normed for a population applying to selective schools) match up with their percentile scores on tests like the ACT and SAT (normed for much larger groups). I'm also tracking the projections from kids' 8th-grade EXPLORE to 10th-grade PLAN to senior ACT scores, just (naturally) as the ACT folks are about to change their whole system. (Quick takeaway: Individual classes do seem to have their own collective character, confirming ages of teacher instinct.)

It is work worth doing, even if we're still in the shallow end. It helps us see whether we are doing as a school what we claim to be doing, and whether there are kids or groups whose performance differs from the generality of our students. We've now offered the CWRA for three years, and in time we hope to start making better use of the results from that, which seems to measure capacities we say we focus on.

Earlier this week we administered the High School Survey of Student Engagement, the HSSSE, through a joint effort of Indiana University and NAIS. The HSSSE has the advantage of being easy to give and to complete, not terribly expensive (about four bucks a kid for us, using the paper version and including the reports), and of providing a picture in the moment not only of how engaged students are with school and their work but also of their lives as students in our community. It'll be interesting to see what we learn.

I'm confident that we are learning something in all of this, but I have to remind myself to take a deep breath every time I spot a provocative trend or what looks like a disturbing anomaly–the sky is not falling, and few data sets amount on their own to an *Aha!* moment. But there is definitely stuff we can use to make our school a better place.

What keeps me grounded as I burrow around is my constant awareness that our sample sizes are small and that each little number represents the efforts of a person. Public school teachers, parents, and students have begun to resist against the waves of standardized testing that seem to be transforming public schools into giant data-collection sites. The testing regimes under which kids and teachers in many places live is a vacuum sucking the heart out of education and processing alleged evidence of student learning—bubble tests on end—into nothing more than numbers that can be used not only to "prove" almost anything but also to dehumanize the students into data points—even as they are the ones whose time, energy, and anxieties feed this monster. No wonder dystopian fiction is so popular with kids these days.

No, kids are not data points, neither at my school nor anywhere else. The minute anyone at a school loses that distinction is the moment when someone needs to start questioning this whole data thing. Kids are kids, and the data they offer us—especially from limited, snapshot instruments like the HSSSE and standardized tests—is at best a poor measure of who they truly are and what they will accomplish in the fullness of time.

Not Your Father's School, May 8, 2014

46

THE BLAME GAME: ELITE COLLEGES AND STUDENTS' DOUBLE LIVES

It's been a tough summer for "elite" colleges—those eight or ten or twelve schools whose names everyone knows and about which everyone has an opinion. I suppose these schools should be pleased that their brands, or at least the collective "Ivy League" brand shared by eight of them, are so well established that when someone, especially one of their own like William Deresiewicz, takes a swipe at them, so many other heads start nodding.

The critique as I've read it takes up yet another strand of the anti-intellectualism that has probably been noted in American culture at least since the election of Andrew Jackson and was given a label in the 1960s by Richard Hofstadter. Colleges are just too elitist and their self-centered students too focused on goals other than the welfare of democracy—and on top of it they're just way too expensive to be worth the effort and time and money and debt. It's true—trust me here as a tuition-paying parent—that the cost is bordering on the insane.

I confess right here to being a product of a couple of these schools, as are a couple of my kids. So when I read the screeds against the careerism and unquestioning adherence to highly questionable values of which students at these schools are accused, I admit to getting a bit defensive. Heck, I'm pretty much just a schoolteacher, not an investment banker, and my kids seem most likely headed for not-very-remunerative niches in the world of education, so I know that not everyone at these colleges is slavering to become a hedge fund manager or a zillionaire tech entrepreneur.

But as someone who works and has been a college counselor at a Northeastern sub/urban independent school, I can see that there are plenty of things in the system of which inquiring minds ought to be critical. But I am not sure that slinging mud at Ivy League students as a body is going to provide much of a solution.

It's the first day of faculty meetings at my school, and we've already heard our head's overview of what promises to be a pretty exciting year, consolidating some recent curriculum initiatives and re-thinking some of our key spaces, functions, and practices. The goal here is to provide a better education, a better experience of learning and being, for all the kids in our relatively diverse student body. It's about school, about pedagogy and curriculum and values, about reaching and challenging and engaging kids—all the good things we expect and for which we entered this profession.

And so our students will soon join us and proceed through the year. They will study, write, take examinations, listen, debate, collaborate, play on teams, act, make music, make art, make friends, and otherwise be adolescents experiencing all the good things to be had in a pretty rich educational environment. From our educators' vantage point, they will be engaged in worthy work whose end is largely in itself— education in the liberal arts and in meeting the challenges of growing up. At graduation, we will look at these children and we will probably conclude that it has been a job well done.

But "the culture," including the world of many of our students' families and friends, imposes on our students another agenda: to leverage every morsel of the school experience toward the very tangible goals of selective college admission and, especially since the Crash of 2008, a high-income career. We at school think that we are asking students to explore opportunities for leadership because it is a way of becoming "all one can be." But many students in schools like ours have people who are effectively their "managers"—sometimes family members, sometimes independent counselors, sometimes "strategic" friends—for whom every leadership opportunity is a résumé item that can pry open the college admission office door just a bit further.

Now, as schools we're not naïve, and we understand that this is a part of what we do and what we are (and why we have college counseling offices, of course, and why we publish, often with a sigh at the necessity as well as some secret pride, our college-admission lists). But I really don't believe that my colleagues here first and foremost think of ourselves as being in the business of polishing little darlings for prestigious college admission or luscious careers. We know that what we do is seen this way, and we don't much like it.

But we do tend to acquiesce to this dualistic world, in which we practice and try to live by our ideals even as what we do is seized on and packaged and occasionally trashed by others as being part of some kind of game—what one of my own children referred to as the Beauty Pageant for college admission. We believe that a student's transcript and letters of recommendation are true snapshots of a person, while to the rest of the world these are tickets, sometimes lucky and sometimes not. Yes, it's icky.

In a very real sense many of our students live double lives, on the one hand the developing learner and on the other the applicant-in-training. It's perhaps no wonder that so many students who find themselves having meet with extreme success in the college admissions sweepstakes struggle with the reality of actually being at one of those "elite" colleges. It's also perhaps no surprise, with all those managerial adults cheerleading their successes through childhood and high school, that so many of these students have a hard time stepping out of this double life to figure out who they really are and what they want to be.

It must also be said that there are plenty of very able and ambitious students for whom their desire to do well in class and to lead, play, act, and serve in all those extracurricular activities is 100% authentic. For more students than the critics admit, admission to a hyperselective college opens the door to wondrous, happy, deeply experienced opportunities; these kids aren't all careerists, sheep, grade-grubbers, or empty husks.

I've spoken out here and elsewhere about the need for schools to do the things they say they do, and I have to say I hear most schools expressing their beliefs in learning and growing rather than attaining. But the attainment message is there, sometimes between the lines and sometimes spoken out loud because a school feels it must, and it isn't going to go away. It takes a brave school to say it doesn't care about these things, but the very statement is kind of its own antithesis.

But rather than make fun of or hate on the students who are victims of this double-life syndrome, whether they live it or choose to live it themselves, shouldn't the critics perhaps be paying more attention to the messages that the media—including much of the pundit class in and out of the academy—and society at large send to parents and kids and schools starting long before anyone has started filling out the Common Application?

Isn't the fault far more in ourselves, in the world we have created or let be created, than in the academic stars whose successes we both celebrate and, when the mean spirit moves us, deride?

Not Your Father's School, August 25, 2014

47

IN WHICH I CONFESS TO LACKING GRIT, APPARENTLY, AND BLAME IT ON FAMILY

The most exciting place I knew growing up was the "everyday" living room of my grandparents' house. It was just across the street, so I could go there whenever I wanted.

The room also served as the main reading room of the "library" that was their house, the room where the bound set of Thackeray and the Dr. Eliot's Five Foot Shelf of books added a certain leathery patina and smell. It was also the room where I could explore the books my grandfather had acquired over the years in response to his serial enthusiasms of the moment. There were textbooks for dozens of languages, books on various facets of engineering and on photography, books on nature filled with gorgeous color plates of *The Apples of New York* and *The Fishes of the Great Lakes*, or maybe it was the North Atlantic. There were even a few books on sports, golf in particular.

I didn't ever know my grandfather terribly well, as he was in ill-health for much of my sentient childhood, and I never heard him say it, but he was quoted by those who should know (that is, by students and teaching colleagues, the folks for whom he saved his best thoughts) as having proclaimed, using the words of G. K. Chesterton, that "A thing worth doing is worth doing poorly."

What a shocking line from a respected educator! But yet, he had a point that I fully and completely embrace: that one doesn't need to be a past master, a single-minded obsessive, a ninth-degree adept to enjoy doing something or learning about it. The Expert may be an American icon, but there is no reason that someone should have to be fluent in, say, Dutch to be interested in it as a language or to memorize the scientific names and characteristics of every apple in the Empire State to appreciate the glory of upstate apple-ness.

For my grandfather, this dilettante's approach to learning a few things (and sometimes more) about quite a lot of things was a source of intellectual and emotional joy. He wasn't interested in throwing his knowledge around at cocktail parties, although I daresay he might have unintentionally done so; he just liked learning stuff.

Of course, we live in an age when we are told that persistence, mastery—grit!—is the *sine qua non* of meaningful living. We're told to devote our lives to whatever matters to us, to repeat as necessary (and The Gladwell has decreed that 10,000 times are necessary), until we have broken through the barriers of weakness of character and failure that leave those less gritty lying in the dust. Poor sad souls.

So there was my grandfather, child of immigrants and a college scholarship boy who gave up his chance to be a doctor in order to become a Latin teacher (thus alienating himself from his parents forever and aye). At the age of forty he chucked a steady teaching gig to start his own initially wobbly school. He would score low on the Grit Scale. Poor, sad, quixotic soul.

I realize that my own household has taken on some of the characteristics of that living room; my Amazon account and my forays into the world of library book sales, where my spouse is a disciplined shopper and I buy like a sailor on a spree, are all the proof anyone would need to convict me of having inherited my grandfather's lack of grit.

So, Gritless Wonder that I must be, I find myself considering that the whole "grit" thing might just be more than a little over-blown. The recent critique that has been waged in the blogs of educators I admire seems to be onto something, suggesting as it does that prescribing persistence for victims as a band-aid for systemic social failures is more than just a little bit facile and cruel.

There's grit, and there's grit: heavy-duty, damn-life's-torpedoes streetwise stubbornness versus good do-bee persistence—and what educator isn't for persistence when it matters when it comes to schoolwork? But an educator I worked for once noted, that "sometimes giving up in a no-win situation is a sign of intelligence." There are students who have been dealt hands that no amount of extra effort on homework will turn into winners; grit alone won't do it, and the mental and emotional energy to sustain this kind of grit are a price that no child should have to pay, although of course many do. I think that we need to focus more on fixing the no-win situations than on worrying about who has grit and who doesn't.

The point of my grandfather's saying, I think, is that in the end a thing worth doing is a thing worth doing. Sometimes we may achieve full mastery, and sometimes we can only do the best we can. Whether we're up for 10,000 repetitions, or whether we just want a taste and then to move on, his belief and mine are that curiosity and enthusiasm are felicitous starting points for the exploration of a world of wonders.

I'd rather have my recollections of poking around in my grandfather's library than be under the compulsion to prove how much grit I have. I think, old-school teacher that he was, that my grandfather would agree.

And as for the grit enthusiasts among us, let's keep in mind that there's a difference between persistence and heroism, and that we oughtn't to be demanding heroism from every disadvantaged kid—at least until we're ready, 24/7, to demand it from ourselves. Let's focus not on heroism, nor grit, nor "accepting no excuses," but rather on something we can all own to.

I offer up what may be a rabbit hole of others' thoughts on this matter <u>HERE</u>, and I would humbly direct readers to Laura Deisley's comment and her citation of <u>Science Leadership Academy</u> and EduCon founder Chris Lehman's call for an "Ethic of Care" in response to what Laura beautifully describes as kids' "yearning for relationship and purpose."

An Ethic of Care beats grit all hollow.

Not Your Father's School, February 2, 2014

48

THE PLAYING FIELDS OF ETON—AND 21ST-CENTURY WATERLOOS

I have been thinking quite a lot about branding and independent schools lately, and I am hereby decreeing that the most enduring tagline ever created about our schools is that attributed to the Duke of Wellington: "The Battle of Waterloo was won upon the playing fields of Eton."

The line has a suspect provenance, but that doesn't really matter. What matters is the way in which the sentence encapsulates by implication all the virtues that elite British manhood required to defeat Napoleon and, in time, ensure that the sun would never set upon the Union Jack: courage, stoicism, resourcefulness—all the qualities of the student-athlete and ultimately the warrior, suitable indeed for the century and the situation.

Which has me wondering, at the end of a globally discouraging winter, what the battles of our century will be. Right now all the forward-thinking educators I hear and read seem awfully fixated on the vocational skills and workplace attributes enumerated as "21st-century skills" by various employers and business councils, and I am assured that subtle technological proficiencies in social media and other Web 2.0 skills will guarantee success to our students in the world of the future. They will need these skills to conquer global warming and spread health care, peace, and prosperity around the flattened globe. Some of them will be the next Bill Gates or Steve Jobs, changing lives with beautifully designed products that are solutions to problems we never knew we had.

It's a lovely picture, progressive in its optimism and focused on the things that education is supposed to be preparing kids for: college, jobs, and responsible citizenship. This is all good, and I'm all for it.

But maybe it's time to take a cue from the past and ponder the kinds of real experiences our students are having in our 21st-century schools and whether we are serving our students well with either our programs or our platitudes. Will our schools prepare students for the battles—and I use the term here in all its meanings—they will face in our century?

The hundred years that followed the famous victory of Wellington and his schoolmates saw the expansion of European empires and European democracy, but millions— of people died in their wars of conquest, oppressive colonial regimes, and the revolutions that brought the Industrial, Imperial Age into being. While sun-kissed heroes of Western Civilization like Wellington, George Armstrong Custer, and Kipling's <u>Stalky</u> pulled on their boots and primed their guns to spread Victorian blessings, European families as well as indigenous communities from Alaska to Arabia to Afghanistan to Australia saw their lives and worlds shattered.

The dawn of the 20th century saw a new version of the elitist avatar, and prep schools worked to embody "muscular Christianity" in their missions and practices. The new heroes were Dink Stover and the Rover Boys, privately educated in the glories of the Strenuous Life, somehow combining the best qualities of Jesus and Theodore Roosevelt. (This version of the prep school hero managed neatly and ironically to ignore the authentically strenuous lives of the majority of teenagers of that era who left school at age 12 or 14 and worked in agriculture, resource extraction, industry, or urban commerce.) The poets of the British trenches and the novelists of the Lost Generation provide us with all too many autopsies on the body of values and beliefs drummed into schoolchildren a century after Waterloo.

Those who survived the trenches and could sublimate their bitterness and cynicism soldiered on into the Great

Depression. Their children, of the generation of Phineas (in *A Separate Peace*) and Holden Caulfield, either missed World War II or they became the scheming and ironical Mr. Roberts or (a bit later) the self-righteous, over-bred crew of the U.S.S. *Caine*, deeply affected by but eluding the worst consequences of the war that killed not only 417,000 American soldiers but also as many as 70 million people worldwide.

Ahead of us in 2010 we have global climate change, an exploding population demanding access to shrinking stocks of global resources, and a backdrop of terrorism and war with a daily death toll that would appall us if we paid attention. Political civility even in old and established democracies is seriously on the wane; crazies who fly their airplanes into tax offices are cheered as martyrs, just like religious fundamentalists who blow up marketplaces. The rest of this century could shape up into something distinctly unpleasant, and we need to be educating people who can help pull the world out a real nosedive, not just earn a living by their cleverness and sophistication.

On one level, and I'm not ready to linger here, screeds on the irrelevance of the breathless TED Talks are pretty much beside the point. What schools need to be focusing on, along with the effective use of social media in the classroom, is how to provide experiences that are like the playing fields of Eton—experiences that will bring forth (or instill, if you are Old School) the best qualities of resourcefulness, critical analysis, courage, and committed engagement that will prepare students for a world that could look more like that of *Mad Max* or *Blade Runner* than *The Jetsons*.

I'd actually look well beyond curriculum and pedagogy here. Wellington (or whoever) didn't cite the classrooms of Eton, and I suspect that character—real character: values, courage, optimism, even faith—is still largely a product of advisories, of discussions of school and social values in dormitory common rooms and club and activity meetings, of chapel talks and school meetings, and—yes—of athletics.

Society's needs, though, have moved beyond a stiff upper lip or muscular Christianity. We're going to need innovative thinking and the ability to face large-scale, immediate, and even horrific problems—to improvise, lead, and endure when cyberwarriors bring down the Internet, when resource wars threaten to engulf both developing and developed worlds, or when violence becomes a regular aspect of political disagreement even in our own communities.

We're also going to need empathy, not just for our own warriors and compatriots but for all the "others" who comprise our complex world and even for our enemies, who perhaps understand us a willfully poorly as we understand them.

Where are we teaching our children how to confront challenges on this scale? Where are we even admitting to ourselves and our children what the future might look like if things go wrong?

Neither Wellington's teachers nor his coevals could have foreseen the struggle against Napoleon, and the faculty and graduates of St. Grottlesex in 1938 didn't understand that America would soon be battling the forces behind the Anschluss and the Rape of Nanjing. What calamities and existential challenges don't we foresee, and are we truly giving our students what they will need to face them?

Admirable Faculties, March 21, 2010

49

WHAT'S DANGEROUS ABOUT THE GRIT NARRATIVE, AND HOW TO FIX IT

There's been a great deal of buzz lately on the topic of grit. As educators we're all for persistence, resilience, stick-to-it-ive-ness—the stuff of grit, right? But it turns out that there's grit, and then there's the way some people are talking about grit.

Because there has been a bifurcation of grit, a tidy split in the word's connotation that came about so quietly most of us, to our embarrassment, missed it until we had our noses rubbed in it by sharp people who figured out what was happening. (Educator Ira Socol offers a stinging summary of this critique here.)

On the one hand there's what we have always understood grit to be, a set of dispositions and habits that incline a person—a student, in our world—toward staying with a problem, toward fighting through a challenge. Good stuff, and indeed a quality of character that is pretty much unexceptionable in any circumstance one can imagine. The history of our nation, from persistent Pilgrims losing half their number in their first Massachusetts winter to doughty little Abraham Lincoln walking all those miles to borrow and return books to obsessive Thomas Edison testing a million (or maybe it was fewer) substances to find the best material for the filament in an electric light bulb. *Apollo 11! Apollo 13! The Miracle on Ice!*

But no good deed goes unpunished. Place this exceptionalist and triumphalist narrative of the overcoming hero against the reality of our society, and the lights of success shine even more brightly against the backdrop of our failures. Move the lens closer, and we find ourselves gazing at high levels of poverty and underemployment—the eighty percent of our population who among them only lay claim to seven percent of our national wealth—while at the top a single percent have commandeered forty percent. Four-fifths of us are losers.

Thanks to our if-you-keep-folks-agitated-they'll-keep watching-your-show media and the never-ending ululations of "reformers," many with (in)vested interests in their own brands of corporatizing and privatizing school reform, we are a nation obsessed with education and a pervasive sense of institutional failure. In this atmosphere, what could be easier than to create a dire narrative tagging the poor and underemployed by their obvious association with schools that underperform?

The poor, underemployed losers are losers because they attend lousy, underperforming schools. The problem for the "reformers" and their conservative supporters, however, is that this narrative locates the blame for this cascade of failure on social conditions: systemic poverty, even (gasp) racism.

Saved by grit! What observers are now calling the "Grit Narrative"—that anyone can succeed if they just work hard enough, try hard enough, keep their nose to the grindstone and endure whatever travails life throws at them—provides a perfect solution. The poor who stay poor lack grit! The students in underperforming schools lack grit! Their parents lack grit! Even their teachers are shiftless, gritless slugs, protected by unions when they're not taking long vacations. No need to worry about poverty and racism—those are just excuses. The real problem is an endemic lack of grit, individual failure writ large across whole populations.

I just returned from the annual conference of the National Association of Independent Schools, where the topic of grit arose here and there amid some pretty interesting sessions on school leadership, school change, and how we keep the ship of education moving forward. And independent school teachers, perhaps contrary to what you might believe, are a pretty liberal and tender-hearted crew, as anxious to make our schools welcoming, inclusive places as teachers anywhere. Diversity and social justice have been on our minds for a while.

Thus it made sense that a number of the featured speakers at the conference had stories to tell that drew on experiences of working through poverty, dysfunction, and racism. Astronaut and scientist Mae Jemison, Walgreens executive Stephen Pemberton, and John Quiñones of ABC News moved us deeply with their stories; great people, conquering long odds, who grabbed your heart and held on.

But I couldn't help thinking, as I listened, that to some degree we were setting ourselves up to co-opted by the Grit Narrative: here were men and a woman who had beaten the odds and emerged from humble backgrounds to lives of influence and purpose, the very exceptions to the grim rules that the Grit Narrativists love. Quiñones, Jemison, and Pemberton made no excuses; they have overcome.

In a relative sense, it might be too easy to hear our speakers' stories—and I don't think for a second that they themselves would ever imply or believe this—as a critique of their peers for whom urban poverty or the foster care system or prejudice remained insurmountable obstacles. The Grit Narrative condemns the poor by implication as it celebrates the success stories.

As educators we have to catch ourselves sometimes. I applaud Jemison, Pemberton, and Quiñones and admire their courage, character, persistence, and nerve, but I can't let that admiration obscure the fact that our schools—all of our schools, public and private—are part of and to varying degrees both victims and sustainers of a system that distributes resources and power in staggeringly inequitable ways. We cannot ignore the reality that poverty and racism correlate with educational underperformance at levels that simply give the lie to the Grit Narrative.

For hundreds of years our society allowed skin color and economic success to serve as facile proxies for the content of a person's character, and for a long time I was pleased to think that in my lifetime we might be getting beyond that. How wrong I seem to have been; the Grit Narrative, its shadow spreading back over the land under the guise of "research," threatens to take us straight back to an era where poverty is about laziness and where failure, unless it's the "failing up" of a revered entrepreneur, carries the stain of moral bankruptcy.

A few years ago some researchers brought the old-timey word grit back from obscurity as a smart descriptor for certain positive qualities. It is now time for these same researchers to step forward and reclaim their word from the demagogues who are turning it into a code word as pernicious as anything from the era of Robber Barons and Jim Crow.

Grit is good, but the Grit Narrative needs to go back to the nineteenth century and stay there.

"Independent Schools, Common Perspectives," *Education Week*, March 3, 2014

50

IN A DYSTOPIAN WORLD, A COMPELLING CASE FOR INDEPENDENT CURRICULUM?

A colleague observed the other day that the recent proliferation of unusual essay and short-answer prompts on the applications of super-selective universities might have a purpose other than making 18-year-olds commit to a decision on their favorite movie or what, exactly, inspires them. The colleague's hypothesis is that these colleges are packing their applications with such provocations—interesting as they may be—against the day when "affirmative action" is overthrown by the Roberts-Trump court.

When affirmative action goes, argues the colleague, colleges at the apex of the admission food chain will abandon their requirement for applicants to submit standardized test scores in favor of asking students to impress (and perhaps even entertain) admission readers with their arcane tastes in films—*Mr. Blandings Builds His Dream House*, anyone? (and yes, I have seen this as a student's choice)—and witty responses to clever questions. The very colleges that the Testing-Industrial Complex was built to serve will send "double 800s" the way of the dodo.

The basis of the idea is that the most forceful arguments put forward by those who oppose affirmative action are always based on quantitative applicant data. Every test score, every Grade-Point Average, every tally of Advanced Placement courses on a transcript, becomes a metric by which students can be objectively ranked for admission or rejection. This is the argument put forward by many activists who maintain that high-scoring Asian-American and international students, for example, are seriously underrepresented at selective universities. This is the argument that the families of many bright students use against the advantages conferred by legacy admissions and "athlete preference."

Get rid of all the numbers, a college might be willing to say, and we'll focus on the subjective, personal data that we collect through our smart applications and school and teacher recommendations—à la the varied application prompts <u>Tufts University created some years back based on Robert Sternberg's work</u> on the nature of intelligence. (Perhaps along the way colleges could even get rid of the annoying checklists that are an optional part of standard teacher recommendation forms.) And while we're at it, get rid of class rank and GPAs.

Coincidentally, I believe, some leading and forward-thinking independent schools have already been taking steps to get away from numbers-driven programming. Since 2002 a number of independent schools, including Phillips Exeter Academy, have ceased to offer classes with the College Board's trademarked "Advanced Placement" designation. No one can count the number of "AP" courses on an Exeter transcript in order to make a comparison against an Andover or New Trier High School transcript; Exeter has made the case for its own high-level courses, and colleges get it. No Exeter student is disadvantaged by not having taken courses that their school doesn't offer. Nor are students from Riverdale Country School, Crossroads School in California, University Liggett in Detroit, St. George's (the Rhode Island one), Westtown, or Lawrenceville. Or Beaver Country Day School, Fieldston, Christchurch School, St. Mark's (in Massachusetts), or Sandia Preparatory School—to name but a few.

Many independent schools gave up reporting student class rank to colleges years ago, on the premise that in a class of 50 or even 90, individual ranking points don't mean much and that ranking inevitably led to unhealthy competition that corroded schools' communitarian cultures. Colleges scarcely blinked.

Currently a-borning in the independent school community is the <u>Mastery Transcript</u>. Being developed by a consortium of schools that happens to include Andover and Exeter, the Mastery Transcript is an effort to replace grades as we know them with a more descriptive and fine-grained descriptive articulation, possibly on multi-dimensional continua, of skills that the student has mastered, supported by evidence of actual student work that can be examined and adjudged by college admission officers. No grades, and of course no grade-point averages.

All of these practices—score-optional admission, doing away with class rank, eliminating Advanced Placement-designated courses, and the grade-less transcript—are the darlings of the some of the most advanced thinkers in contemporary education, present company humbly included. They see each of these as supplanting current practices that contribute to a numbers-driven, competitive, and unhealthy culture of learning whose instrumental values displace relevant curricula and de-value creativity, deep critical thinking, and—broadly—whole-child learning.

How ironic, then, or perhaps cleverly strategic or maybe just inevitably right that these very practices could soon coalesce somehow as the centerpiece of a "new and improved" system of college admission whose single goal is to obliterate the power of quantitative data after the demise of affirmative action. Colleges say that they are looking for creativity, multiple perspectives, and a vast range of skills and interests, and, absent test scores and GPAs, the schools that have embraced the idea and practice of independent curriculum and assessment, often in forms that are still a bit radical in 2017, will be preparing students to present applications that truly reveal the personal qualities and authentic skills that colleges say they desire and may be consciously positioning themselves to elicit when the numbers have to go.

There's a caveat here, however. If this is indeed a strategy, it's a strategy that appears to be emanating from elite colleges, and the "creative" questions that I have run across so far seem perhaps too comfortable to my own white, male, middle-class self. The minds that will be developing application forms in years to come will need to design prompts and provocations free from cultural bias; if the intent is to use idiosyncratic prompts to develop diverse classes, these can't feel too much like extensions of familiar bourgeois parlor games. This will call for the kinds of research on validity and reliability across cultural and gender lines that Big Test should have been conducting on all its multiple-choice questions all along.

And how even more ironic that the right-wing reactionaries who must hate every one of these radical new educational ideas might be the very people to force their wide adaptation as part of an "affirmative-action-free" college admission process.

Cleverness, diversity of perspective and experience, critical analytical skill, and authentic engagement with real-world problems: imagine a student cohort whose members bring these skills and qualities to their college experience and couldn't care less about the one right answer on some silly test.

Not Your Father's School, December 17, 2017

51

CODING IS JUST THE NEW SURVEYING

A tip from a wise friend, Thomas Steele-Maley, brought me back to some old school reading the other day: Theodore Sizer's *The Age of the Academies*, from 1964.

A look at the roots and fruits of the pre-Civil War "academy movement" in the United States, the little volume begins with a long essay by Sizer in which he describes the academies, their successes, and their ultimate failure and demise. His theme is that these quasi-private, generally exurban, comprehensive, largely boarding, and highly idealistic and idiosyncratic schools deserve a larger place in educational historiography. Where once I read this book as just an opportunity to fill in some gaps in my knowledge, I now find myself reading with a more focused, or maybe just older, eye. I was struck by a couple of curricular aspects of these schools, in particular the presence of surveying and navigation as fields of study.

When I made much of my living teaching United States history I often found myself struck by the role of surveyors in our past; I even read a few books about them.

Famously, George Washington started his career in this profession, and two British surveyors named Mason and Dixon left a lasting legacy with their eponymous opus magnum. As a kid growing up in the <u>Holland Purchase</u> and not far from both Holland, New York, and the intersections where the Two Rod and Four Rod Roads meet Big Tree Road in Erie County, New York, I was aware that all that we call home in this country was at some point measured and parceled out by surveyors and their land-speculating counterparts.

I also grew up with a fascination for the sea, and it had been impressed on me that the former student at my father's school named Nathaniel Bowditch was named for the ancestor who had authored in 1802 _The American Practical Navigator_, a compendium of knowledge and advice that no doubt saved any number of mariners from leaving their bones on the ocean floor.

Navigation, like surveying, is a branch of applied mathematics, and, like surveying, it was an essential skill not only in measuring and mapping and getting from place to place but also in establishing the infrastructure for the American economy. Maritime commerce, like land speculation and sales, was essential to creating the wealth that allowed the young Republic to survive and thrive. And, like surveying, navigation was frequently a part of the curriculum of many of the little secondary schools that grew up in the American hinterlands as academies in the first half of the nineteenth century.

Sizer notes in the opening essay of _The Age of the Academies_ that even in that era there was a kind of schizophrenic attitude toward education, particularly the parts of it that concerned "practical" or life skills versus what we would today call the liberal arts—the study of history, language, and literature. Academy founders and supporters seem to have made their peace with a kind of dual curriculum, one that included things like surveying and navigation (and often bookkeeping) to fit young scholars for practical work and the other more bookish, to raise the level of discourse and discernment among the nation's future active citizens.

Of course we have the same push-pull today, in almost identical terms and strangely similar forms. The epicenter of the discussion in our time lies around yet another branch of applied mathematics, computer programming.

Coding, _Edudemic tells us_, is "the job of the future," and hordes of educators, employers, and parents seem to concur. However well our laddies and lassies may be able to analyze _The Great Gatsby_, greet their Quebecois neighbors in French, or understand the causes of the Civil War, they must also be able to bend the power of the CPU to their will by cannily issuing a few commands in one or another of the technical languages known as "code." (In an article in *Independent School* magazine I explored the rise, or re-rise, of coding—which many of us learned in rudimentary form decades ago—and some of the motivations and methods behind the increasingly urgent movement to teach coding in our schools.)

As one who is interested in the coding phenomenon and something of a supporter, despite my misgivings about the pre-vocational nature of some of the pro-coding rhetoric, I find myself taking comfort in Sizer's little essay and its reminder that there is a recurring theme—an applied-mathematical recurring theme, no less—in American education just as there is a recurring, or more likely constant, dichotomy in our thinking about what secondary schools should teach and, in a more broad sense, what they should do. Coding is simply the new surveying, just as I suppose was the "New Math" as it purported to help us catch up with the Soviet Union in the Space Race/Missile Gap era or was basic electrical theory in the Age of Edison, Marconi, and Tesla.

Poor mathematics (and physics)! Destined always to be the Most Important Thing in one form or another, and equally destined to be the thing that so many children and adults find hardest to master. But I shall leave the Why of that to better or more mathematical minds than mine.

I think seeing coding as the new surveying is actually helpful in putting all the hype in perspective. I would also point out that the primary practitioners of surveying and navigation and coding were usually just the employees of the folks who earned the real fortunes, though there are certainly those who managed to master both the technical and business sides of the enterprise: walk around any New England seaport town and take a gander at the lovely homes built by some of the whaling and merchant captains, masters of navigation as well as seamanship.

Until something comes along to change the American nature, I suspect there will always be the push-pull between the practical and the, er, what, the beautiful? the spiritual? the impractical? in American education. But at least we've been grappling with this problem for a couple of centuries, now, so the fact of the apparent conflict seems less alarming. The only alarming thing to me at the moment is the shrill, relentless voice of economic anxiety and the presence of potential tools that could more or less erase the non-"practical" from the curriculum entirely. I personally think this would bring about the dystopia posited by Fritz Lang in *Metropolis*, and I don't want it.

I like the push–pull we have and that we've had just fine, thank you, and I like thinking that it's a matter of history and not some contrived "innovation." I also like knowing that I am walking a path once trod by Theodore Sizer on his way to the *Horace* books, the Coalition of Essential Schools, and another "little" book I love dearly, *The Students Are Watching*. There's still more to be learned from *The Age of the Academies*, and I'm happy to give some more time to learning it.

Not Your Father's School, November 23, 2014

52

THE NEW RELEVANCE

When I was in college nearly 50 years ago and when I started teaching a few years later, "relevance" was the hip byword, but I have to say that relevance matters even more nowadays. Relevant in 1970 meant "familiar and connected to my own experience"—all about ME and how I am feeling about things—but today there is a new relevance, something far deeper and more critical—and far less about ourselves.

Our world's a mess, and we have been doing an increasingly good job of making students aware of this, even if our pop-culture consumer society has offered them the handy drug of materialism to numb the harshest realities. But I believe that we are currently witnessing, sometimes against a backdrop of bigotry and insensitivity, a new birth of caring, empathy, and desire to become involved.

Most students, I think, are more or less ready and even happy to engage with the world and its problems, which is why environmental clubs and service learning programs and international trips just keep growing, even when college admissions officers tell us they roll their eyes at such things. It's also why schools have lately been brought up hard against their own students' expectations for inclusivity and social justice. Kids want to make a difference, they want to be relevant, and they want their learning to be relevant. For today's young people relevance is about building connections between their ideals and dreams and the world's challenges—figuring out what they can actually do about the mess. Relevance in their education is learning more about the mess and how the skills, content, and understandings they gain in the classroom can help them play a role in the clean-up.

Unfortunately, relevance is often understood to be one half of a dichotomy whose other side is "academic content coverage."

We can blow up the syllabus in an elective, maybe, but we can't spend too much time on terrorism in AP World History because the exam is looming nor on travel bans in U.S. History because maybe it's April and we still have World War Two and the Cold War to get through. Teaching compound interest with examples from the mortgage and housing crisis might be a great idea, but it adds a layer of complexity and time. So does looking at the physics, say, of earthquakes, tsunamis, and hydraulic fracturing ("fracking") at a time when the human and economic sides of these topics could infuse every classroom minute for an entire school year.

The **New Relevance**, which is what I call this phenomenon, faces outward. It's not about our lives and the lives of our students but about the world we're living in and going to live in, about seeing issues not from one's own perspective only but from the prospect of being engaged social and political actors. Conservative or liberal, secular or faith-driven, we might all agree that our students will need to know how to act, to do, to judge, to advocate, to lead, and to support on a whole variety of issues that are becoming less remote and more real, more vital, sometimes more frightening, every day.

The **New Relevance** makes the lens of experiential reality, of engagement, essential to the way we teach—the way we teach everything. In the **New Relevance**, "depth over breadth" must be the mantra for curriculum in every area. After all, we've been reading for a decade that the nations that whip the U.S. in high-profile international tests teach fewer topics in greater depth in the very subject areas in which our schools look most pitiable.

The depth–breadth issue has a human manifestation that is worth thinking about. Tim Brown, head of IDEO and de facto guru of design thinking, is a passionate believer in what he calls the "T-shaped person," one who has tremendous depth of knowledge and skill (the vertical stroke) and equal breadth (the crossbar) of vision, emotional intelligence, cross-disciplinary understanding, and collaborative capacity. Step back and squint, and you can see the outline of the T-shaped person in the expressed ideals of most mission-driven schools. In the past we have perhaps largely depended on our athletic teams, dorm life, clubs, and spiritual exercises to teach toward the human side of that breadth, but today we ought to be invoking the principles of the **New Relevance** and "21st-century learning" to embed it firmly in classroom learning, as well.

I also want to say that secondary schools should be energetic in giving colleges a chance to put their money where their mouths are on the **New Relevance**. This means that we ought not to be afraid to be more experimental in our programming and pedagogy. Ask schools that have done new and different things, and in every case colleges will have voiced enthusiasm not only about the nature of the new student experiences but, more importantly, also about the idea that these experiences will differentiate students when their files are part of a stack of applications. Even more radical changes may be coming—the work of the Mastery Transcript Consortium promises to be epochal—but most of our schools could be finding many more interesting ways to express their missions and values in ways that would make their students look less like products of some prep school cookie cutter.

Students whose educational experiences have been built around the **New Relevance** in its many manifestations will be as well equipped as anyone on the planet to get us out of this mess. Starting right in our classrooms, let's students' their hunger for a better world by intentionally and comprehensively playing our parts in the **New Relevance** and giving them the tools and skills to build it.

The Independent Curriculum Blog, June 6, 2017

LIVING OUR VALUES

It's overused in my peer group, but I like the word "authenticity" a whole lot. I like the idea of things that are what they are, linoleum floors and Klondike bars and traditional Roman Catholic Masses, whether or not I want them in my life. The most immediately and forever-after helpful advice I ever received as a teacher was to "be myself" in the classroom and around the school, and when I first encountered Grant Wiggins's work on "authentic assessment," it was a breath of the freshest air I had inhaled in education.

Just as an experiment, find a school mission statement that resonates for you, and then, starting from scratchy, build a school around those words. Imagine yourself, in that imaginary school, being your authentic self in a school inspired by those stirring words and constrained by nothing in making them come true for students, each of whom is also inspired and nourished to discover and become their own truest and best selves in this school built on ideals.

That's really all that I am asking of independent schools here.

53

BEING WHO YOU ARE

A recurring moment in my life as an overnight camp administrator for many summers was when older campers and staff—often "lifers" who had been campers and moved on—declared in some comfortable setting that "camp is the only place I can really be myself."

I never actually went to camp, but I could sort of relate: there was a month each summer when I could be myself as explored the space around my grandparents' place, mostly free of the structures and judgments of growing up among teachers on a school campus.

The past couple of conversations on the #PubPriBridge Twitter chat have been inspired by the very general topic, "K–12 Education and Summer," and there have been moments that brought the whole idea of "being yourself" back to me. One of the questions with which we wrestled, in general, even global terms, was the whole idea of school responsibilities for students during the long summer break.

Most schools take one or another approach to summer reading, from gentle, almost laissez-faire programs with "suggestions" to hard-core requirements that build toward some kinds of assessments for accountability in the fall. Over the years I've worked with both, and generally, as a reader first and as an educator second, I have been disappointed. The light-touch systems don't seem to create more engaged readers, and the heavy-handed systems manage to build most students' (and to be sure, many parents') antipathy toward coercive summer reading that is often assigned as almost a medicinal measure, like a dose of castor oil, ostensibly to counteract learning loss and the slipping away of habits of mind.

The #PubPriBridge chat participants didn't dwell on the summer reading question. Rather, we found ourselves asking bigger questions about things like "student interest" and equity. "Research says," we are told, that summer slide is lower for kids on the higher end of the socioeconomic scale, and certainly many more affluent students have more opportunities for summer enrichment of one sort or another, including summer camps and family travel. Teachers of younger students (to generalize from a small sample) are more inclined to want summer to be a time for kids to develop or follow their own interests, while teachers of older students are more likely to fret about academic loss. We're keenly aware that summer jobs, once a staple of student growth across the socioeconomic spectrum, are harder to come by; grown-ups now need to work year-round in low-paying jobs that kids in summers past could take or leave.

Whatever the requirements schools do or do not place on kids during summers, most students continue to live in an asymmetrical world, where summer break is very different from the school year. I'm not sure whether a change is needed, or which side of the equation—the way we construct school or the way we construct summer—ought to be modified if we deem it desirable to figure out how to make kids' live more holistic, or consistent, or whatever we'd want to call it if we wanted kids' lives (and maybe our own) to be less about contrasts and more about "being ourselves," year-round.

This all got me musing on the origins of my grandfather's school. Reports from a century ago have him as something of a martinet as a schoolmaster, a man who ran a taut ship. But in the summer, starting sometime in the early 1920s, he began a tiny summer "camp" in which he explored how he might teach the boys in his regular classes whom he was beginning to identify, with the help of a neurologist named Samuel Orton, as having dyslexia.

By all accounts—and there aren't many of them—this summer camp/school was idyllic. Boys lived in tents, had lots of time to mess around in the woods, and had plenty of one-on-one time with their teacher, who at least worked in his shirtsleeves instead of all three pieces of a woolen suit. The few remaining photographs show happy men, young and old, and we know that from this experience grew the teaching methods that were to become in a few years the centerpiece of the program of a new—also tiny, at first—school. There must have been something magical, no doubt in part because my grandfather genuinely liked and believed in his students, who must have figured this out as they worked, studied, and played in the woods at the foot of what became the school's ski hill. In any event, something was working.

In *Mindstorms* Seymour Papert writes of the samba schools in Brazil, which he presents as a kind of model learning environment where "learning is not separate from reality" and where the intentionality behind their establishment was collective and natural: "They were not made. They happened." I wonder now about that little summer encampment where a teacher tried to figure out how best to teach dyslexic boys, and what those students/campers felt about learning and reality. There was a teacher, more at ease than in their school building and certainly more focused on their needs, and there were the pleasures of life when they weren't being tutored.

They were in tents, not their comfortable city mansions, and one imagines that their daily responsibilities differed considerably from their pampered home lives. But some of them went on to work at the school in later years, and one married the teacher's daughter; there must have been something in it.

I wish I knew how to offer each kid something that met his or her own needs or fed his or her particular interests each summer. I wish that opportunities were equitably available to all kids and that every child might have a safe, resource-filled environment in which to make the most of their long summer breaks as experiences for growth and learning—

different from "school" or like it, as they might prefer—that would carry them forward with the best kinds of momentum that the school year can support. I wish, in other words, that we could put more of our energy into considering the nature of summer, and its meaning for students (and for teachers, of course), as a time when individual, whole-child needs might be met just as we aspire to meet them during the academic year.

If wishes were fishes...

But the #PubPriBridge conversations at least began to clarify for me another aspect of that "<u>Whole-Child Education for Every Child</u>" dream that serves me as a mantra, a goal, and perhaps a promise. However we manage it, we ought to give every child the chance to know, and to be, who they are, 24/365.

Not Your Father's School, June 11, 2014

54

GIVING MEANING TO INDEPENDENT SCHOOL MOTTOS

No prep school movie or TV episode is complete without either students decked out in crested school blazers or a shot of some preposterous granite-edged entrance way sporting a school motto, always in Latin.

However much and for whatever reasons we may venerate the idea of Latin, the anti-intellectual strain in the American character is immediately put on guard by words we don't understand, and words in a foreign, dead language (apologies to the Vatican and Latin teachers everywhere, who like to tell us that Latin is an immortal language) possess mystical power: they may be absurdly pretentious, but *Dude, they're in Latin!*

I have written quite a lot about the aspirations of independent schools, and how these are ultimately the expressions of schools' founders, usually idealists for whom embodying a philosophy of education into a school of their own creation was an act of extraordinary hope. (Today we can discern this in the founding sentiments of many of our most interesting, idealistic, and philosophically compelling charter schools.)

The schools I've been at have a varied group of aspirational mottos, from (in translation) *"Truth"* (in Classical Greek, actually) to *"Bear and Dare"* (as in, "endure and be bold;" both liberal translations of the Greek), *"Work conquers all,"* and *"From the mind and by the hand."* The work motto seems appropriate for a boys' school founded by a famously stern pedagogue, while the mind/hand phrase is just right for a school founded to realize John Dewey's ideal of active, creative learning.

The one of my schools' mottos that needs no translation is *"Play the Game,"* which lends itself to all kinds of ironic or cynical interpretations. In fact, it comes from an 1897 patriotic poem by Sir Henry Newbolt in which a nervous young soldier is recalled to his duty by being reminded to "Play up! Play up! And play the game!" as he had in his school days. The poem was still stirring souls when this particular school—then for boys only—was founded in 1923.

The most oft-cited independent school motto is *Non sibi,* or "Not for oneself," the venerable Latin phrase used by Phillips Academy, better known to the world by its location, Andover (Massachusetts). Like many, it's terribly easy to be cynical about, but consider the school's founding moment: 1778. A great many New Englanders were pondering the balance of self-interest and altruism from many perspectives, some of them exceedingly perilous. Paul Revere himself created the school's seal, in the 1780s, after the peace had been won; not a bad little historical moment. (And yes, of course you can raise the perspective that in the Revolution the middle class merchants of New England had brilliantly co-opted the farmers and other working classes to help them shed an annoying tax burden and allow themselves to pile up even larger fortunes. But it wasn't that simple, really.) I like that Andover keeps its motto front and center (there's even a <u>Non Sibi Day</u>), signifying an ongoing conversation of just the sort we all need to be having.

I am also pleased by the motto of the fascinating Lick-Wilmerding High School in San Francisco. An avowedly "private school with a public purpose,' the school's motto *"Head, Heart, Hands"* (in English) seems apt for a school with roots in vocational education that today is seriously college prep and equally serious about ethical development and civic engagement. I like as well the motto of a girls' school that merged into what was to become Lick-Wilmerding in the mid 1900s: "To do things uncommonly well."

It is unusual and unusually heartening to come upon a school whose students both know the school's motto and use it regularly as a touchstone for their lives. The boys of Fenn School in Concord, Massachusetts, know that *Sua Sponte* (official school translation, *"On one's own responsibility"*) carries with it <u>the sense of taking ownership of their own learning and behavior</u>, a nice touch of self-reflective meta-teaching accomplished simply by the reiteration of two short words; an equally effective reminder to children just entering adolescence that their words and deeds have an impact on others.

In the end, what we all have to work with in order to have our own impact on others are our ideals and our willingness to see them through. We've all seen enough television and movie dramas in which someone is reminded of those ideals and goes off, in a heroic climactic moment, to enact them and conquer whatever iniquity has been driving the plot. All we can do as educators is to keep our ideals, like Andover's or Fenn's mottos, front and center—and then do what we can to support ourselves, our schools, and our students in living up to them.

"Independent Schools, Common Perspectives," *Education Week*, April 15, 2013

55

THE HIGHER CALLING: MISSION-DRIVEN SCHOOLS, DUTY, AND (PUBLIC) SERVICE

This is about words that can sometimes sound out of tune to the contemporary educational ear, but words that we have heard often lately in important contexts: duty, obedience, service.

When I hear these words, I tend to envision uniformed men, rigid countenances, shiny weapons. At first blush, they sound a bit too much like some kind of servitude, submission even—restrictions on the liberties I value most despite their sometime associations with those who defend these very liberties. In my mind, at least, my work and life stand for freedom of thought and expression, to a critical questioning of creeds and codes.

But the other day I had a small epiphany about schools, and in particular (not surprisingly) about independent schools and their leadership.

School mission statements, as I've stated probably too often, serve as both foundational and aspirational documents, and along the way I may even have used the word "credo." From such statements flow values and legacies and daily practices and even—in culturally well-ordered schools—legacies. At least in theory, those who comprise the living communities of a school operate under the guiding principles set forth in the mission and developed within its frame.

Might this not mean, on a level that seems absurdly idealistic but may not be at all, that to some degree school communities are bound by their mission(s and values and similar statements of belief and intent) in the same ways that other enterprises are bound by creeds and codes? If such statements of belief and intent are to be used as touchstones or even litmus tests for the evolution of school policies and practices, as current approaches to accreditation essentially require and as I and others continually urge, then is there an element of "obedience" or "service to an idea" or even "duty" in the idea that a school's words and deeds should uphold the ideas for which it purports to stand? When we talk about fit—for a student, for a family, for a faculty member, for a trustee—are we not also talking about a certain devotion to those ideals that requires a constant consciousness of thought, word, and action?

I'd not want to be accused of being a strict mission constructionist, a mission originalist, or a mission fascist; the interpretation of mission is as subject to social, cultural, and educational evolutionary forces as the Nicene Creed or the United States Constitution. Recent years have seen way too many individual and group actions, supposedly based on obedience to one idea or another, that have deeply and often violently wounded the human family and stood in the way of what I want to believe is our common purpose to love, to live, and to prosper together. School missions must never (if ever they have been) be written or enacted to do harm.

The idea of school mission statements probably has its origins, like so much in Western education, in the monastic codes and Rules of the European Middle Ages. Where monks and nuns once "submitted" to such rules, under the guidance of abbots and abbesses, teachers, administrators, trustees, students, and families now gather—bound by various contracts—to live out school missions, to interpret and enact and experience their meaning within an evolving cultural milieu and an ever-expanding understanding of the ways in which children learn and in which effective learning occurs.

But I think it is not too far-fetched to suggest that school leadership, at least, might be said to echo monastic practice of a past age. What is a school head, if not someone who agrees to both live by and to further the aims set out in the mission statement that forms the centerpiece of the "hiring statement" hammered out by a Search Committee? Are there not in this role elements, although almost never described as such, of duty, obedience, and service?

Who and what, though, are being served? As one of my bosses has stated as his personal credo, "Schools are for kids," and this higher purpose must both underlie and transcend even the most idealistic of mission or values statements. Whatever ideas and ideals a school embraces have the ultimate purpose of supporting students in the service of their growth into fully realized and capable human beings—"the best versions of themselves," as I and others like to say. And however much we find ourselves in "customer service" mode when we deal with families, it is a more estimable purpose toward which we are working: we would all acknowledge that our "duty" is not to satisfy every whim or demand of families and students but rather to achieve what we sometimes describe as our "higher calling"—to bring out the best in children and adolescents.

For what it's worth, I sometimes wonder whether schools' tendency to focus on their practice these days—to present themselves in the marketplace in terms of specific "new and improved" methods and tools used in their classrooms—might undervalue this higher calling. Day-to-day practical issues and the loftiest of aspirations are hardly antithetical to each other, but sometimes it's easy to forget that the one ought to reference the other if we are to maintain integrity, in all senses of the word, in our work.

So I think it's not so far-fetched for us at least occasionally to consider our work within a framework of duty, obedience, and service. If this sounds atavistic, then so be it. I believe, however, that education, formal or otherwise, is a human duty that the experienced have to the less experienced, a service that the older (and perhaps wiser?) perform for the younger. It's a human thing, and if we put some values behind it all, why should it not take on a philosophical or even moral cast, something like obedience to principle?

And then of course there's the yet-higher calling of our schools themselves, to take their place in the battle against not just ignorance but injustice, not just illiteracy but inequity, not just apathy but amorality. No, we're not a uniformed service, but it might not be such a bad idea if every now and then we considered that we might be not just employees and educators at one independent school or another, but public servants of a public good.

Not Your Father's School, January 10, 2015

56

STRATEGIC THINKING AND—SCHOOL THERAPY?

Over the past few years I have found myself moving in circles that involve school advancement as much as the teaching-and-learning side of the house. Here I have been made privy to both the anxieties of independent school leaders on matters like enrollment and fiscal sustainability and the solutions—or at least the paths toward solution—that schools in our time are embracing. On the one hand there's the matter of branding, recruitment, financial aid, and enrollment management, while on the other there's the bigger question of strategy and of setting of priorities beyond the moment.

Tiffany Hendryx of Firebrand, a friend and a professional brand-and-marketing guru with whom I occasionally partner on various projects, has noted that much of her work in these areas these days is taking on the character of what used to be called "strategic planning." My complementary observation has been that a thoroughgoing school self-analysis and marketing study makes many of the same demands on a school as the traditional self-study and committee visits that are part of school accreditation.

Alas, the legacies of both "strategic planning" and "the accreditation process" frequently have much in common: both are big-deal productions with lots of players, lots of effort and disruption, and lots of lofty language and good intentions that all too often result in reports that live out their days in dusty binders or thick, yellowing file folders, unconsulted and unremembered as the urgencies of each successive moment determine the actual course of the school. All the hard work and high hopes are soon forgotten, or remembered just enough to breed ruefulness or (much worse) cynicism.

The observation that Tiffany and I have shared is that a full-on, serious, intelligently and thoroughly undertaken marketing or branding effort—call it what you will—grabs a school's attention and generates real action far beyond a "strategic plan" or accreditation. I suspect that this is because the marketing effort has a significant and easily identifiable price tag, beyond the consultant fee of a traditional strategic plan or the incidental dollar costs and uncalculated human costs of accreditation. A board allocating several (or more than several) tuition-equivalents toward helping the school find itself and its external market is likely to pay more attention in the long term to the recommendations of that effort than to a complicated report written in consultant-ese or education-ese "for internal use only."

The more sophisticated the people in the "marketing" world become, the more they understand and can speak the language of schools and education to those for whom this is a first language, just as they can speak the language of advancement and "business" to those within schools whose concerns are either external or operational. The best "marketers"—and I keep using quotation marks because this term seems both inadequate and too freighted to express what I really mean—have enough knowledge of trends in educational best practice to assess what their clients are doing and might be doing, or doing better, in their classrooms. This all goes to the simple mantra of know who you are—say who you are—be who you are, the fundamental goal of any school, to deliver the experience it promises. The very best of these programs offers schools a manifold path toward this goal, which ought to be the holy grail for every school.

Tiffany and I have occasionally joked that this work needs a new and better name, beyond even strategic marketing or even strategic thinking. "School therapy" comes to mind but is probably a dog that won't hunt because of its negative or "deficit" connotations. But the idea is to help a school understand itself more deeply and then adjust both its internal behaviors—programs and policies—and its external presentation—the so-called advancement functions—to become the whole and integrated institution that it purports and believes itself to be, acting on those propositions and beliefs consistently and to the very best of its ability. If those aren't the goals of therapy, I don't know what are.

New models of strategic thinking are taking form, some fast-track and short-horizon and others, like the "zero-based" methodology developed by our friend Grant Lichtman, making rigorous demands on school personnel to examine their own practice and purposes in the most fundamental ways. All of this is to the good, toward the improvement of the independent school breed if you will, and it can only help schools find ways to serve students in better ways.

Based on my own experience and my contemplation of what could yet be, I am a fan of the idea of bringing a school's external face and internal life together, to create an iron-bound relationship between what a school says and what it does that is both harmonious and honest. As families look for schools that can match their dreams for what their children might become, it's going to be more critical with each passing week that schools know how to communicate what they offer and how then to offer what they communicate. If it takes a little therapy to help a school to achieve this, it's time and treasure well spent.

As a kind of epilogue I'd offer one more thought: That the school that is truly doing what it says it does is going to be a happy place. The ruefulness or cynicism fed by the knowledge that a school's rhetoric has hollow spots or that its programs aren't all they could be evaporates when words and deeds are brought into authentic alignment. Happy, confident teachers and administrators make for happier students and families, and we all know what that means to a school's true "brand" and to its future.

Not Your Father's School, July 31, 2014

57

TEAMWORK AND GRACE

I found myself in an interesting conversation yesterday with a coeval—in fact, a high school classmate.

We were watching a hockey game involving our distant alma mater, the unlikeliest of fans and the unlikeliest of alumni lettermen in this sport—I the one-time manager and he the statistician. But there we were, sitting companionably in a warm room overlooking the rink, enjoying the game.

"How wonderful," he said, "to be on a team, with all that good feeling and that sense of common purpose and common identity—all that spirit."

Which is of course why we were there, having felt in our schooldays that same sensation to whatever extent such ancillary beings as managers and statisticians can.

But that feeling of common purpose, at its most exalted, in those moments when one's own identity is subsumed in that of the group and its purpose, is a rarity, I suspect, for most of us, even when we're teamed up for work or fun.

I recall years ago discussing the concept of sin with a Unitarian clergyman. Sin, he explained, is a turning of one's back on community. Grace, he went on, is the embrace of connectedness and community. As an example, he suggested the moment in the 1980 Winter Olympic hockey tournament when the United States defeated the Soviet Union. What millions felt as they watched that game wasn't political jingoism or sports partisanship—it was an uplifting of the spirits as we shared for a few instants the transcendent exhilaration of those young men's impossible triumph, the victory of their spirit; for a few moments we shared and held that spirit. That, said the minister, was grace, the gift that humans are intended to understand, dimly, as an intimation of an immortal, ineffable force for good.

I can't say that my friend and I experienced grace yesterday; in point of fact the game ended in a slightly disappointing tie. But I was reminded of why we join together in communities as schools and why we sometimes ask students—and why they sometimes ask us—to join together in teams, groups, and ensembles for work and play. It's not just about lessons from sharing tasks or duties or learning to mesh our efforts with those of others. It's certainly not about winning or losing, good grades or bad, although there are powerful, even transcendent, lessons to be learned from these.

In the end, it's about that feeling, whether it's a divine gift or just a lovely aspect of human social psychology. We work together, strive together, and sometimes even suffer together because through this conjoined experience we may, on rare occasions, know the joy and shared identity that can only come from a common endeavor, deeply purposed and deeply felt.

I find myself mourning on a spiritual level for students in schools where exigencies of time and limited resources have pushed leaders to drop programs in sports and the performing arts. I sorrow for students prepping frantically, pushed by terrified teachers, for mandated standardized tests for which each child sits alone and where individual scores exist only as data points, where there are no teams, only aggregates.

Where, I ask, is the grace in that?

Not Your Father's School, December 30, 2013

58

LOOKING INWARD, LOOKING OUTWARD: GOOD FOR US ALL

A large part of my personal life these days is a kind of distillation of what it has been for a while: advancing the work of independent schools. I've got threads going relating to curriculum and assessment, data development, professional development, even marketing. It's all pretty fun, and incredibly rewarding.

But there's something else that's been on my mind for a while that doesn't obviously align with my other projects. Paradoxically, it might yet turn out to be the weightiest, and it has taken mild-mannered me into realms where emotions can run very high.

Just as I believe that independent schools and their faculties need to break down the barriers among themselves, I have a strong conviction that the independent school community needs to step outside of itself and engage as a productive force in the national conversation on education and teaching. I even happen to believe that independent schools ought to be natural allies of traditional public schools.

Why? What's in it for independent schools, especially in a time when demographics have some schools teetering even as changing approaches to teaching and learning demand that all schools, teetering or prospering, evolve in ways that are famously "disruptive." How does adding my voice to a discussion that is often contentious advance independent schools and the independent school community?

My logic comes as much from my heart as from my head here, and it's actually pretty simple.

From ages four to twelve I was a public school kid, a happy kid in a half-rural, half-suburban community. We lived at the ill-defined confluence of three school districts, and my parents chose what they chose; alas, I missed out on being able dine out forever on my days in a two-room schoolhouse, which really was one of the options.

I've written elsewhere and in some detail about the experience, but the long and the short of it is that I had pre-kindergarten, kindergarten, looping teachers, smallish classes, a rich menu of the arts, recess, P.E., and even Spanish—all during the Eisenhower presidency. It was pretty idyllic, as "Leave It To Beaver" as anyone could ask, small-community post-war America. We took Iowa tests in the spring and received the results with our final report cards, to be opened in the car on the way home and challenging my parents to explain percentiles.

A couple of years back, being sometimes slow on the uptake, I realized that the very programmatically similar kindergarten and elementary education my own children were receiving in suburban Boston was actually different from my own in one rather critical way: their independent school charged a boatload of tuition, reduced considerably by the fact that my spouse works in the school. What had been free for me, and an experience not dissimilar from that of lots of kids in the U.S., was in fact now a luxury item, paid for by tuition at a school with selective admissions. I suppose we could move to a town with ritzier public schools, but that would mean paying taxes that would amount to a luxury tariff that we couldn't possibly afford.

Because by this point I was paying pretty close attention to what was happening in public schools across the nation. Testing was becoming not an assessment but a burden on which schools in poorer districts "underperformed" and had funding cut and teachers punished. The thoughtful, orderly, holistic kinds of teacher evaluation I promoted in independent schools were being supplanted in public schools by a quick look at aggregated test scores—which every bit of research proves are correlated on the lower ends with poverty just as they are at the higher ends with wealth. And socioeconomic stratification was only making this worse. Things like arts, languages, and recess were being slashed in the name of test preparation.

Charter schools offered (and may still) promise, but their results seem as varied and uneven as their missions and business models; and some of these business models were designed to extract profit from a system that was already being cut to the bone.

My Southside Elementary School idyll was being transformed more and more, as I look at it, into a kind of public education nightmare (Gerald Bracey called it _Education Hell_), with kids, who are supposed to be beneficiaries, often looking like victims—not to mention their beleaguered teachers, whose drop-out rate seemed to be rising with that of students in many areas and is rising still.

It didn't look right to me as I allowed the picture to come into focus, and it doesn't seem right now. I decided it was time to start talking about it.

I'm proud of, often awed by, our schools and by my colleagues in them, and I believe that we have something to say in the national conversation on education. Setting aside the politics of it, which I would really like to do, I think we owe it to our fellow citizens and their children to share what we know about teaching and learning and to encourage our public school counterparts to share with us.

Along the way I don't see any reason why our profile as a sector shouldn't rise, but for real reasons, based on authentic evidence of what we know about teaching and learning and kids (which is a treasure trove) rather than just on reputations and self-serving elitist lore. I believe that people will always need and find our schools, and I believe that most of us in this business are sincerely committed to figuring out how to make our schools more accessible to more families and more kinds of kids. If we became nationally renowned for our contributions to the enterprise of education rather than for the Dun & Bradstreet ratings of our alums, what could be bad about that?

And so, I see my work and activities these days as actually making up a unified whole, a whole still devoted to independent schools and to bringing out the best in them— not just for self-promotion but because it's our civic duty to connect and to share.

And that's why I'll keep going to EdCamps and why I participate in the #PubPriBridge Twitter chat, even as I hammer away at projects ranging from marketing to promoting the Independent Curriculum Group. Looking inward is fun and deeply interesting, but looking outward, scary as it can be, is the challenge that is icing life's cake.

By the way, the transcript of the inaugural #PubPriBridge chat is online; please check it out and embrace the spirit.

Not Your Father's School, January 29, 2014

BEFORE D-E-I: INDEPENDENT SCHOOLS' QUEST FOR A LANGUAGE AND PEDAGOGY OF EQUITY AND JUSTICE

These four essays made up a series that ran in my "Independent Schools, Common Perspectives" blog in Education Week *in the summer of 2013. They represent my attempt to explain— not as an apologist or an advocate—the general nature of the work around what we now call Diversity, Equity, and Inclusion that I had observed in my half-century as a student and staff member at independent schools. The essays are doubtless incomplete and are by definition affected by my own biases. I present them here as a slice of a history that has yet to be comprehensively written, surely by a better-placed and better-informed observer than I.*

59

DIVERSITY AND MULTICULTURALISM: THE INDEPENDENT SCHOOL STORY—PART 1

In 1988 the National Association of Independent Schools published and began to support its Multicultural Assessment Plan—the fabled MAP. The idea was that schools would follow the Plan to complete a comprehensive self-assessment of their spot on the spectrum of multiculturalism and diversity. It might have seemed a little late, twenty years after Dr. King's assassination and at least as many years into many schools' efforts to do what the Civil Rights Movement had been all about, at least in its inception: integrate.

Integration is an old fashioned and rather awkward word these days, but at least through the '80s it was still in regular use as part of the "busing" controversy. Decades after Brown v. The Board of Education, public schools everywhere were still working at—and populations north and south resisting—decreasing the levels of segregation and trying to proportion their student bodies to reflect the makeup of their whole communities. It wasn't pretty; we have all seen the 1976 photo of the African American man on Boston's City Hall Plaza apparently about to be speared with an American flag during an anti-busing demonstration. (It supposedly wasn't exactly like that, but close enough, and the image endures.)

Some independent schools had been "integrated," to the extent of having a handful of underrepresented minority students, for decades, but in the late 1960s and early 1970s, many more turned their attention to this aspect of their student bodies. Maybe because teachers tend to reside on the leftish side of the political continuum, many began to push their schools toward something more than monocultural admission and financial aid policies. Slowly—by the mid 1980s in many cases—school pictures began looking a bit less like slices of Wonder Bread and a tiny bit more like, well, America. Faces of color were still relatively sparse, but they were present. Schools paid close attention to and perhaps disproportionately trumpeted gains in their minority enrollments.

Fairly quickly it sank in that a more diverse school photo might be a good thing in a highly abstract way, but that diversity alone—especially if largely confined to the student body—was not going to ensure a school's becoming the "multicultural community" its viewbook promised. The mere presence of students of color might change a few things— many of them out of sight of the adults in the school—but it did not a community make.

The next wave of change was curricular. The literary canon of works by "dead white men" and triumphalist historical narratives began to give way, in many places, to reading lists offering real diversity of voices and to approaches to history partly informed by counter-narrative perspectives from the likes of Howard Zinn, Ronald Tataki, and even Eric Hobsbawm.

The 1980s were yeasty times for history and English teachers, as we re-learned our fields from new points of view and tried to re-cast our courses to include different voices and cultural perspectives. It should be noted that women's history and a "feminist" perspective—thanks in part to the work of Carol Gilligan, some of which was carried out at an independent school for girls—were a part of this curricular revolution, appearing just as Title IX and new attitudes towards girls and sports were also spurring the formation of new teams across the independent school nation: girls' soccer, girls' lacrosse, girls' ice hockey. (And the debate goes on at some schools, whether to call these "girls'" or "women's" teams. When I coached I let my teams decide, and against my Sensitive New Age Guy hopes they invariably opted for "girls'".)

What was missing was a concerted effort to understand what the experience of being in a white-majority school filled with relatively affluent and socioeconomically privileged kids was actually like for the newly arrived students of color, some of whom were beneficiaries—and all of whom were often maddeningly presumed to be beneficiaries—of schools' expanded financial aid policies. Since many schools also had mandatory athletic programs, where students of color who performed well were subject to the double stigma of being presumed to be on "athletic scholarships"—and a few, to be sure, had been recruited for just that reason. Socially, too, it wasn't uncommon for students of color to be omitted from invitation lists and excluded from certain in-crowds.

So the NAIS Multicultural Assessment Plan of 1988 showed up just in time, offering those schools who undertook it a cutting-edge (for the time) instrument for measuring and evaluating the success of their efforts to multiculturalize. The self-study was rigorous and in most schools rather painful, revealing area after area in which things could be much better. A subsequent report by a trained visiting team of MAP veterans from other schools—the Plan's culminating stage—tended to be more painful still. The mirror didn't always reveal what schools wanted it to, but then they had asked for it, and most took the results to heart.

It should be noted that of the thousand or so NAIS member schools at the time, perhaps fewer than ten percent underwent the MAP. It was costly to complete, it was hard, and it was guaranteed to reveal large and embarrassing shortfalls between good intentions and actual outcomes. But many of those schools who did were soon in the first phalanx of the movement toward becoming more truly diverse and "multicultural" communities, in which the initial step was the establishment of offices and administrative positions focused on this very work. In the next decades these offices would work toward moving schools forward toward better work and toward helping faculties and students—underrepresented minorities as well as majority—navigate the difficult waters of access, address the uneven distribution of privilege, and begin to build authentic mutual understanding.

In the next couple post I will write more about independent schools and their ongoing struggles to move from "diversity" to true inclusivity. No school can claim to have "finished" this work, but many are on the journey.

"Independent Schools, Common Perspectives," *Education Week*, July 26, 2013

60

DIVERSITY AND MULTICULTURALISM: THE INDEPENDENT SCHOOL STORY—PART 2

By the mid 1990s some scores of National Association of Independent Schools member schools—out of a thousand—had completed the Association's Multicultural Assessment Plan. This was a poor showing, by most measures, but the existence of the Plan and its support by the Association indicated a growing understanding of the challenges of creating multicultural communities from hitherto pretty homogeneous independent schools.

One common recommendation of the MAP was the establishment of an office or at least a point person within the school to lead ongoing work and to serve as a central clearinghouse for issues that might arise in day-to-day life. This was a great deal to ask of any one individual—to be at once ombudsman, professional development leader, spokesperson, mediator—but "diversity coordinators," "multicultural deans," and "directors of diversity" began to show up on administrative lists at independent schools across the country.

There was resistance, which ranged from concerns over cost to worries that focusing too much on the situations of underrepresented minority students put undue pressure on them to a principled—or double-speak, as some regarded it—attitude that since this was clearly the work of everyone in the community, creating a special office would relieve people of a shared responsibility. In schools where the minority population was still very low, the need wasn't always clear, as if white students were to be excused from understanding difference if little or no difference was immediately apparent in their worlds.

The question also arose of other kinds of historically oppressed status. Sexual orientation and gender expression were also present as issues of diversity, as were religion, cultural heritage, and even just plain gender—many of these comprising "invisible minority" status. From the perspective of "the work," though, most schools tended to focus on race, the mantra being *"If you can talk about race, you can talk about anything."* While this didn't always satisfy as a response, it was certainly true that jump-starting candid, open conversations across racial boundaries proved to be hard work, with scary but critical opportunities to consider issues of identity development, cultural capital, assumptions of every kind, and matters of skin and class privilege. Developing capacity in these did make other kinds of conversations easier, in time.

The designated leaders worked their hearts out, and many were able to bring their communities to places in which honest conversations could take place and in which teachers understood more about the lives and challenges of their students—and increasingly their colleagues—of color. Kids seemed to internalize these new capacities faster than adults, but it was still usually the naïvely racist utterances of students—assumptions voiced in class, comments made unthinkingly, humor or terms repeated from television or music—that could bring whole institutions to a halt and inspire teach-ins and emergency meetings at all levels.

How to respond to these moments became part of a larger discussion. Should the school have "diversity days" or events, or do such things relegate big, systemic issues to one-day's consideration? Celebrate or even acknowledge Black History Month, or does doing so in one month imply that minority issues don't matter in the other eleven? Visible and emphatic reaction to small incidents, or do you risk building up a kind of "diversity fatigue"? There was never one right answer, but just having the discussions seemed to help—even as it exhausted many of the first generation of independent school diversity professionals.

I am sure there are schools where these conversations seldom took place, for whatever reasons. Although I have heard the words spoken, few schools could legitimately believe "these things aren't an issue here." It may have been, and may still be, true that schools for younger students, in the early stages of their own racial identity development, may not experience in as obvious ways the turmoil that can occur in middle and secondary schools, where both majority and minority adolescents must come to grips with what it means to live and work in multiracial communities, sometimes with palpable extremes of socioeconomic diversity.

This might be a good time to point out that for many people in schools where this work became a focus at the turn of this century it was a time of the highest hope and idealism. One of the little privileges that independent schools can claim is that they can aspire to be small utopias built around their loftiest ideals. In the middle of earnest, highly focused work on diversity and multicultural education there is a point where one can begin to envision one's school as a place where, if we work hard enough and do it right in every way, we can in fact create a truly multicultural mini-world in which we can acknowledge and, yes, celebrate difference and live up to a set of values that transcends the endemic racism, sexism, and homophobia of the outside world. Enter the schoolyard, and forget for a while about the evils of the outside world. It's quixotic, naïve in its own way, but a glimmer of what school could really be—and even of a better world.

I can't speak for schools where this work didn't take place, but I can say from experience that where it did it was challenging, sometimes indeed painful, personally liberating, and important. I don't know for sure that independent schools made more of a point of this—a bunch of them, anyhow—than other sectors of the K–12 world, but I know that for some independent schools and many, many independent school people this was and continues to be the essential work. As individuals and institutions we continue to stumble and sometimes to cast blind eyes, but the work has to go on. Increasing socioeconomic stratification and the struggle of the middle class—reportedly a diminishing presence in independent schools—to keep up with rising tuitions are strong incentives that make the work even more critical if we're ever to build a society whose functioning is not driven by issues of race, wealth, need, and privilege.

I'll be coming back to this topic again, with some observations on where we are as a sector and on how the MAP's current successor, the Assessment of Inclusivity and Multiculturalism, is helping schools continue the work. I'll also be addressing the areas that continue to challenge our schools every bit as much as they challenge our society.

"Independent Schools, Common Perspectives," *Education Week*, August 2, 2013

61

DIVERSITY AND MULTICULTURALISM: THE INDEPENDENT SCHOOL STORY—PART 3

While in recent years many independent schools have been focused program-wise on "21st-century learning" and all its largely technological trappings (along with the professional development challenges these bring), the question of "demographic sustainability" still lies at the core of many schools' anxieties.

It's not just a matter of filling seats at most schools; several decades of grappling with diversity have turned this into an eternal issue. How do we fill our schools, yes, but more critically, how do we create student bodies that mirror, to at least a plausible extent, the demographics of our communities and our nation? This is a question that requires not just the endless game of whack-a-mole that sometimes characterizes life in school, but rather systemic, mission-informed thinking.

As "schools of choice"—people choose us, we choose our students—independent schools have a unique relationship with the concept of diversity. For thirty years and more many schools have chosen to be more diverse, which means attracting a more diverse applicant pool and then convincing accepted applicants to come. As with every question relating to enrollment in independent schools, making this work is conditional around the inescapable fact that most independent schools charge tuition, often lots of it. (A handful, like Christina Seix Academy and the venerable—and lately retrenching—Girard College in Philadelphia, charge virtually no tuition to student families at all, covering expenses through their endowments.)

An independent school's applicant pool and the body of enrollees must, in the end, represent enough revenue for the school to pay its bills. In National Association of Independent Schools member schools last year this included (on average) a financial aid commitment of around 11.7 percent of spending (covering, incidentally, some 22.9 percent of all students). Some schools make much of this up through tuition income alone, although many devote large portions of giving and other non-tuition revenue to financial aid.

There's an ugly reality around money in this country, and that is that not only is more and more of it being concentrated in the hands of fewer families, many of these families are white. Poverty and want disproportionately affect the lives of historically oppressed and underrepresented minority families.

This is not to say that there aren't plenty of well-to-do and at least solidly middle class minority families. But not all these families see independent schools as the best choices for their kids, just as not all white families do. The numbers, then, pretty much dictate that building a more diverse student body is going to have special costs—in recruitment, in building appropriate support for students and families, in training teachers to operate effectively in multicultural classrooms, and in financial aid.

Many schools have risen to the occasion, some spectacularly. There are schools that have made extraordinary strides toward affordability by expanding their financial aid budgets and by developing new formulas (like income-indexed tuition) for the determination of what a family might pay. These schools seem to have found financial practices congruent with their demographic aspirations, inviting obvious questions.

You would be somewhat hard-pressed to find more than a handful of independent schools whose mission and values statements do not contain at least one word like "diverse," "multicultural," "global," "inclusive"—words that, as mission statements are intended to, commit the school to preparing students to live in a world in which everyone is not going to

224

be just like themselves. Some schools even include terms like "equity," "justice," and "community engagement," committing the school to acknowledging, and then presumably preparing its students to struggle against things like inequity, injustice, and self-interest or apathy.

Ideally, the best way for schools to live up to these commitments is to model them, in their programs, their values—and in their own demographics. Teachers, familiar at ground level with the wonders that multiple perspectives can work in classrooms, tend to be especially enthusiastic about this approach, and many administrations and boards are equally dedicated to the diversifying of the student body—and to providing the infrastructure that transforms diversity into multiculturalism and inclusivity.

It's common for educators in our day and age to cite an overabundance of "things to work on" in schools, and currently issues relating to teaching and curriculum tend to occupy the top of most independent school to-do lists. But schools that are truly committed to carrying out their mission not just as places where kids learn academic material but as communities of values are built around shared goals and perspectives understand an omnipresent imperative to do not just satisfactory but energetically excellent work around diversity and multiculturalism, work that serves the direct personal needs not just of minorities of all students and all faculty.

I referred in the previous post to a kind of utopian strain in independent school ideology, the idea that schools are intentional communities aspiring to a kind of social perfection, an admirable if perhaps unachievable goal. Embedded deep in the notion of "mission" is the idea that no school can forget its human responsibilities, even above its academic ones.

And so the work of diversity and multiculturalism goes on, difficult and repeated in endless variation as successive generations of teachers and students pass into and out of schools. We see our society at large make what looks like progress, and we see its terrible failures. Our schools, we believe, must model only the former, although we know that we are bound at times to fail. The belief, the principle, is what must drive us forward.

"Independent Schools, Common Perspectives," *Education Week*, August 5, 2013

62

DIVERSITY AND MULTICULTURALISM: THE INDEPENDENT SCHOOL STORY (PART 4 OF 4)

Education Moves Ahead, as the founding head of my school, Eugene R. Smith, titled his wise and still disturbingly original summary of progressive education in 1924 (and available for free download as an ebook HERE.)And as it moves, it both accumulates things and leaves others behind.

In the previous three segments of this reflective overview of independent school "diversity" efforts over the past few decades I've tried to lay out some of the challenges as schools have seen them and some of their responses. But each year we teach new children, and new adults enter our communities, so in a sense the work we do to build our multicultural communities must be begun anew each year.

There are persistent challenges and new ones that emerge as our understandings are refined by experience and occasional gut-wrenching misadventure. I suspect we will all start school in a somewhat chastened state of mind after the Trayvon Martin verdict; Trayvon could have been our President thirty-five years ago, yes, but he could have been any of our African American students this morning.

However utopian we might wish our schools to be, our streets are not. And recent Supreme Court decisions on voting rights and affirmative action seem to have revived some troublingly pre-Civil Rights Era attitudes. We all have to live with this, but for historically oppressed minorities, these trends have sharp and jagged teeth. And then there's income disparity— the One-Percent versus the minimum wagers to whom McDonald's corporate central lately so helpfully offered budgeting advice, minus things like groceries and heat.

On the flip side, maybe, are the Supreme Court's decisions regarding gay marriage, and how these will affect both attitudes and statutes around discrimination against LGBTQ children and adults. Things seem hopeful, but retrenchment is sometimes only a caucus away. And the profile of transgender and transgendering students is slowly rising, requiring schools to make decisions on topics they have never thought about.

Immigration, reformed or not, has meant an influx into America's communities of new waves of diversity and the need for new or enhanced sorts of services for families and children. Independent schools who truly want to reflect their communities will need to respond; the Dream Act, even in its watered-down form, at least means that in many places undocumented students are not in quite such legal jeopardy as they were a few years back—but financing education beyond high school remains a huge challenge for them as well as for all low-income students.

Many of America's new citizens are Asian by birth or heritage, leaving students and their school communities to wrestle with the "model minority" stereotype and how to combat it. Stereotypes of all sorts persist like layers of old paint on our society, and "stereotype threat," a phenomenon that first hit the national consciousness in an _Atlantic Monthly_ article by Claude Steele in 1999, continues to take its toll on the achievement of African American (especially male) students. (A recent Steele book on the subject, _Whistling Vivaldi: How Stereotypes Affect Us and What We Can Do_, ought to be required reading for every educator.)

And while popular media continue to happily toss off racial and ethnic stereotypes as the basis of music and humor, when kids bring these into the schoolyard things can go sour. The institutional and classroom balance between letting things pass and calling in the "P[olitically] C[orrect] police" remains a tough call, with no right answers and few ever completely satisfied. "The harder we work at this stuff," a colleague once observed, "the better we get at it, and the harder it all becomes."

The work might be hardest of all for schools in areas where there simply is little or no critical mass of demographic diversity; they do still exist. How does a school, or a teacher, create a kind of "virtual diversity," a cultural condition in which participants bring into the room the voices and perspectives of a non-existent diversity? This would seem to be an essential ingredient of a 21st-century American education, but establishing it in a monocultural setting requires intention, skill, and training.

Ten years ago Beverly Daniel Tatum, now president of Spelman College, offered schools an explanation for one puzzling phenomenon in her classic _Why Are All the Black Kids Sitting Together in the Cafeteria? And Other Conversations About Race_. Another candidate for required reading (as it has been for many independent school faculties), this book explores and explains the day-to-day challenges of being part of a minority in a school and offers readers both insight into racial identity development and yet another glimpse of the notion of privilege—who has it and who doesn't—famously identified by Peggy McIntosh in her enduring 1988 essay "White Privilege: Unpacking the Invisible Knapsack." Many of us are still working hard to unpack this in order to become real allies in diversity work and not just politely applauding bystanders.

Early on I wrote here about independent school-public school partnerships and the worthy goals of the National Network of Schools in Partnership. The challenge in this work is to keep such partnerships authentic, with mutual interests served and mutual perspectives aired and shared, and avoid the appearance (or worse, the fact) of old-fashioned noblesse oblige kinds of "charitable service." Here, too, stereotypes go both ways, and working through them is often the first step toward success.

Although the "elitist" tag still smarts, a number of independent schools have worked hard to embed ideas like social justice and community engagement not just into their mission statements but into their programs. If critics view these efforts cynically, the people carrying them out— administrators, teachers, students—most assuredly do not; it's a weak argument to blame kids for the situation they were born into—rich, poor, or otherwise—and a weaker one still to scoff at their efforts to improve their world in whatever ways they can.

In a nutshell, independent schools are what they are, and most now recognize that they cannot be "schools on the hill" but rather must be active parts of their communities, confronting all of the problems and all of the possibilities faced by American society as a whole. Fitfully in some places and with verve and confidence in others, schools are pressing forward. They haven't solved the conundrum of diversity and multiculturalism, but they have worked hard to get a handle on it, to name it and explore it and make it work in the service of their missions and of their students, faculties, and families.

This doesn't mean that independent schools open in the fall of 2013 with any more wisdom or any more knowledge than anyone else. They do open with access to a relatively new instrument for measuring their efforts in the <u>National Association of Independent Schools Assessment of Inclusivity and Multiculturalism,</u> which brings to "the work" the wisdom and knowledge gained in twenty years or so of experience and is supported by a reorganized NAIS office of equity and justice.

And so the work, like education as a whole, will move ahead, with new challenges unfolding, new students eager to create a new world for themselves, and new adults trying to figure out how it all goes together.

"Independent Schools, Common Perspectives," *Education Week*, August 7, 2013

EPILOGUE

Shrill, strident, toothless, misguided. If I haven't been called all of these things directly at any one time, I have probably earned some of them by what you have read here.

Like every "industry," independent schools have their own self-protective reflexes, and despite my having worked at the center of enterprise—as a some-time researcher and writer for the National Association of Independent Schools, for example—I imagine that there are those in the biz who wish that I would take my idealism and my moral distress and my carping blogs and go back to South Wales, New York, for good.

The thing is, that even if I were to do just that, I'd still be smack in the middle of the independent school world, back on the very campus where I grew up. It wouldn't change my perspective one iota.

I love and have always loved independent schools—their promise, their people, the earnestness of the language of their missions and values and profound empathy of their teachers and staffs. I want each of these schools to be the truly amazing place it aspires to be, offering its students life-changing experiences and heartfelt, positive support, and being for its faculty and staff true homes of the heart, a place where each can become the educator and the human they have always wanted to be.

I believe in independent schools, as I have written elsewhere, as Blake believed in the possibilities of England as a new Jerusalem. Sure, some of our schools may still have the history and legacy characteristics of dark Satanic mills, but the best and truest of them are deeply engaged in unceasing mental strife to burnish their programs and cultures into green and pleasant places where their students might launch arrows of desire toward their own best and most idealistic yearnings.

And for America and for our struggling planet, this idealism, if schools can embrace its substance and free themselves to ride their own missions and values as on chariots of fire, offers one more scrap, one more jot, of hope that all of our grandchildren—including, yes, my own grandchildren—might grow up in a finer, more decent world.

www.ingramcontent.com/pod-product-compliance
Lightning Source LLC
Chambersburg PA
CBHW032103280326
41933CB00009B/749

9 781734 247978